MW01621237

Master Choa Kok Sui

# THE ORIGIN of MODERN PRANIC HEALING and ARHATIC YOGA

Transcribed and edited
by Charlotte Anderson

**Institute for Inner Studies Publishing Foundation, Inc.**
Makati City, Philippines
E-mail: iis_publishing_fdn@yahoo.com
Website: **www.pranichealing.org**

Choa Kok Sui
The Origin of Modern Pranic Healing
and Arhatic Yoga/Choa Kok Sui-Metro Manila:
Institute for Inner Studies Publishing Foundation Inc.

First Edition
March 2006
Printed in the Philippines

ISBN 971-0376-07-1

Illustrations by Benny Gantioqui and Jerome Malic
Typesetting by Marie Rose Ramos and Sumakwel Victoria

Published by
**Institute for Inner Studies Publishing Foundation, Inc.**
Metro Manila, Philippines
E-mail: iis_publishing_fdn@yahoo.com
Website: www.pranichealing.org

# BOOKS WRITTEN BY MASTER CHOA KOK SUI

Miracles Through Pranic Healing

Advanced Pranic Healing

Pranic Psychotherapy

Pranic Crystal Healing

Practical Psychic Self-Defense for Home and Office

Achieving Oneness with the Higher Soul

Universal and Kabbalistic Chakra Meditation
on the Lord's Prayer

The Spiritual Essence of Man

Inner Teachings of Hinduism Revealed

Om Mani Padme Hum
The Blue Pearl in the Golden Lotus

Superbrain Yoga

The Origin of Modern Pranic Healing
and Arhatic Yoga

The Existence of God is Self-Evident

## The Golden Lotus Sutras of Master Choa Kok Sui

Beyond the Mind
The Golden Lotus Sutra on Meditation

Inspired Action
The Golden Lotus Sutra on Teaching

Experiencing Being
The Golden Lotus Sutra on Life

Compassionate Objectivity
The Golden Lotus Sutra on Character Building

Creative Transformation
The Golden Lotus Sutra on Spiritual Practice

Achieve the Impossible
The Golden Lotus Sutra on Spiritual Business Management

Possible Miracles
The Golden Lotus Sutra on Pranic Healing

# DEDICATION

This book is dedicated

To my Sat Guru,
Lord Mahaguruji Mei Ling,
His disciples, especially
Chohan Jig Mei Ling
Spiritual Teachers, and Spiritual Beings,

For their Blessings, Guidance, Love,
Help and Protection.

And also dedicated to three remarkable friends:

Mang Dabon, who corresponds to Power,
Mang Mike, who corresponds to Love,
Mang Nenet, who corresponds to Intelligence.

Note: The word Mang means respected sir in Pilipino.

# PRANIC HEALING GUIDELINES

1. Pranic Healing is not intended to replace allopathic medicine, but rather to complement it. If symptoms persist or the ailment is severe, please immediately consult a medical doctor and a Certified Pranic Healer.

2. Pranic Healers are not medical doctors, but medical doctors can be Pranic Healers.

3. Pranic Healers should not make medical diagnosis.

4. Pranic Healers should not prescribe medications and/or medical treatments.

5. Pranic Healers should not interfere with the prescribed medications and/or with medical treatments.

6. These Pranic Healing Guidelines must be posted in all Pranic Healing Centers.

# TABLE OF CONTENTS

# AUTHOR'S NOTE

To practice humility, spiritual disciples will avoid or minimize using the terms "I" or "me". They refer to themselves in the "third person". This is why, in this book, MCKS will refer to himself as MCKS.

Also, when a spiritual disciple achieves substantial oneness with the higher soul and identifies himself with the higher soul, he will also refer to the incarnated soul in the third person. This is why MCKS sometimes refers to himself as "the author" in his books.

M.C.K.S.

* Since the author uses the third person to refer to himself, pronouns referring to MCKS are capitalized. The Editors

# INTRODUCTION

A Spiritual Disciple is guided by four principles:

1. To Think and to Know
2. To Will
3. To Dare
4. To be Silent

For many years, MCKS refused to talk about His personal and spiritual life or His guides in order to practice humility and to practice the principle, *To be Silent.*

To correct wrong information generated by speculations and rumors, MCKS decided to write a biography about Himself, His physical spiritual guides, and the development of Modern Pranic Healing and Arhatic Yoga. This book has been written to clarify certain stories and issues in the mind of the students. It is also intended to share accurate information about His life in order to correct any misconceptions or wrong ideas. He has also compiled information from different people about these remarkable friends.

Spiritual guides play a very important and critical role in the development of the incarnated soul. This issue must be clarified for the students. Just as the teacher in grade school is not more developed or smarter than some of the gifted students, the same may be said for the guides.

Being a spiritual guide does not necessarily mean that the guide is more advanced than a special soul with a very important mission, whom the guide is guiding, nurturing, guarding and protecting.

In the spiritual tradition, a spiritual guide is assigned to an incarnated disciple who has a very important mission to fulfill.

In the Tibetan Buddhist tradition, a geshela or a kempo (one who is higher than an ordinary monk, equivalent to a bishop) is assigned as a tutor to a Rinpoche. A Rinpoche is a reincarnated high lama.

In the case of MCKS, three spiritual guides were assigned to Him to make sure that He stayed spiritually on track, in order to fulfill His mission.

Lord Mahaguruji Mei Ling has been MCKS' Sat Guru since very ancient times, for many incarnations. The term, sat guru, means the permanent spiritual teacher. A disciple has only one sat guru but has many spiritual guides.

All truths are easy to understand
once they are discovered;
the point is to discover them.

GALILEO GALILEI
Italian Genius,
Mathematician,
Physicist,
Astronomer

A time will come when science
will make tremendous advances,
not because of better instruments
for discovering things,
but because a few people
will have at their command,
great spiritual powers,
which at the present
are seldom used.
Within a few centuries,
the art of spiritual healing
will be increasingly developed
and universally used.

A Scientist's View of Man,
Mind and the Universe
by Gustaf Stromberg
Astronomer
Mt. Wilson, California

Chapter 1

# A Very Short Spiritual Biography

Master Choa Kok Sui, at a very young age, of about 12 years old, was already very interested in paranormal and spiritual subjects. For many years, He studied yoga, psychic phenomena, mysticism, Chinese chi kung (the art of generating internal power), Rosicrucian Teachings - Ancient Mystical Order of Rosae Crucis (AMORC), Theosophy, Astara lessons, Arcane School teachings and other esoteric sciences.

Because of His strong interest, He spent more than 18 years researching and studying books and literature on esoteric sciences. He also made close associations with yogis, healers, clairvoyants, practitioners of Chinese chi kung and a few extraordinary persons who *are* in telepathic contact with their Spiritual Gurus. MCKS and His clairvoyant friends spent several years experimenting to determine the effectiveness and the mechanisms of the healing techniques commonly known and used by healers and students of esoteric sciences.*

* Master Choa Kok Sui, Preface, Miracles Through Pranic Healing, 4th ed. (Philippines, Institute for Inner Studies Publishing Foundation, Inc., 2004).

**Grand Master Choa Kok Sui**
Founder of Modern Pranic Healing and Arhatic Yoga
Disciple of Lord Mahaguruji Mei Ling

Chapter 2

# MCKS As A Young Person



MCKS was physically born on 15 August 1952. He has many brothers and sisters. His parents owned several businesses. They were hard working, kind and generous. His father was a Protestant and a thirty-second degree Freemason. His mother is a Buddhist and a devotee of Buddha Kuan Yin. His mother's good friend was a Taoist whom we called "uncle". Uncle was a kind-hearted person who liked to help others and he volunteered his services in a big Taoist Temple.

MCKS studied in Roman Catholic schools up to the university level. At a young age, He went into the spiritual path. He graduated from the university with a Bachelor's degree in chemical engineering. Several of His brothers own businesses. MCKS partially followed His family's tradition by also going into business. Later, MCKS just naturally shifted His focus more toward His Spiritual Mission.

## MCKS As A Teenager

While MCKS was thirteen years old, in His first year in high school, He spent one whole year doing inner purification or character building. Developing the virtues and eradicating weaknesses are very important for aspirants and disciples who are treading the spiritual path. Unfortunately, this is also the most neglected practice by the students. Without the development of the virtues, the disciple will eventually fall.

He also started to practice Hatha Yoga, pranayama and simple meditation. During these years, MCKS learned through direct experience, different methods of how the soul leaves the body either when the body is asleep or when the person is meditating.

The first method is the Roll-over Technique. When the body is sleeping, the soul simply rolls over and out of the body.

The second technique is the Swinging or Pendulum Technique. The soul swings to the left and then swings to the right until it swings out of the body.

The third technique is the Inner Sound Technique. The inner sound becomes extremely loud and the inner consciousness is pulled out of the body through the sound, by listening to the inner sound. The sound is like a very loud buzzing sound, louder than the sound of a jet plane engine.

The fourth technique is the Spiraling Technique. The soul just simply spirals out of the body. The Inner Sound Technique is usually accompanied by the Spiraling Technique.

Almost every night, MCKS would involuntarily experience leaving His body with one of these techniques. His reaction to the initial experiences was that of alarm. Later, MCKS got used to it. The problem was maintaining the continuity of consciousness for a longer period of time. Because of long hours of study, the body was usually exhausted before going to sleep. When these out of the body experiences occurred, He would just simply allow the body to become unconscious so that the body could have a proper rest. All He wanted was for the body to sleep and have a good rest so the body could wake up early and go to school. Even after stopping the practice of the simple meditation, these involuntary out of body experiences continued every night for many years until finally *it* stopped.

## MCKS' Personal Life

When MCKS was in high school, He was living in a family owned building. Although His parents were relatively wealthy, He refused to turn on the air conditioner in His room because He did not want to unnecessarily "financially burden" His parents. He owned only a few pairs of pants which He would wear over and over again until they were completely worn out. Then, He would have the pants patched and stitched and continued wearing them. He did this because even as a teenager, He did not want to waste money and lived a very simple life.

In His university days, He would take public transportation. He did not ask His parents to buy Him a car nor did He ask the family driver to drive Him to school. By choice, He did not ask for anything. He lived an austere life like that of a yogi.

When He asked for money from His parents, it would be for buying books or for paying for lessons from esoteric schools.

As much as possible, MCKS tried to please His parents. He did not argue or talk back to His parents and almost never vocally disagreed with them. If His father wished to see a movie, He would usually accompany His father instead of making excuses that He had something else to do.

## As A Young Adult

MCKS as a young adult had already read and studied many books on healing. He read books on faith healing and shamanic healing and the work on Kahuna healing by Max Freedom Long and others. He also studied and experimented on Rosicrucian healing, on psychic healing books by Amy Wallace and Bill Henkin, by Yogi Ramacharaka, by Benjamin O. Bibb and Joseph J. Weed and others. He also studied and experimented on magnetic healing from books by Abbot George Burke, by Heinz Schiegl, and He also studied *Therapeutic Touch* by Dolores Krieger, Ph.D, R.N. He studied many books on Theosophy, including the *Etheric Double* by Powell, and *Esoteric Healing* by Alice Bailey. MCKS experimented on the different healing arts on His friends, His family, His relatives, and friends of relatives. *Healing at that time was more of an art rather than a science, because concepts, terminologies, principles, techniques and methodologies were non-existent or were not clear.*

In relation to the common people and to ordinary esoteric students, MCKS as a young man, considered Himself as a walking encyclopedia on esoteric knowledge and healing. At that time, He had hardly encountered anyone, physically, whose knowledge was that encyclopedic.

## Experiments on Chinese Medical Chi Kung

In His early twenties, MCKS was introduced to a friend of His mother, who was a real Tai Chi Master from Hong Kong. This person was very humble, amiable and kind. He explained that, when he did healing, he did not point his fingertip at the acupuncture point because it would be too strong for the patient and would damage the internal organs of the patient. Instead of using his fingertip, he would use the pad of his finger to reduce the intensity of the chi energy projected to the patient. He healed patients regularly for many years. It seemed that the Tai Chi Master was unable to train other students to do healing. This is because it requires many years of industrious practice to develop the substantial amount of internal chi energy needed to do regular healing on other people.

Several years later, MCKS' former classmate invited Him to attend a class on chi kung conducted by a Taiwanese Chi Kung Master who studied under a Buddhist monk. The subject matters were:

1. Making the body invulnerable by using simple Chinese Hatha Yoga technique.

2. Circulating the chi energy in the back and front energy channels - again by using simple Chinese Hatha Yoga technique.

3. Gathering of the chi energy to the tan tien inside the navel.

4. The projection of one's own internal chi energy within the tan tien for healing.

For a short period of time, MCKS experimented with Chinese medical chi kung, but He found it *too exhausting*, since the healer was giving his own internal chi energy to heal other people.

This young Taiwanese Chi Kung Master died at a young age. MCKS does not know the real cause of his death.

It is reported that the medical chi kung practitioners in China are allowed to heal only 2 to 3 serious cases per day. For them, healing is exhausting because most of the medical chi kung practitioners use their own internal chi energy.

MCKS' book on Pranic Healing was translated into Chinese in the early 1990's. Based on MCKS' interaction with the Taiwanese Chi Kung Master and many years later with a leader of the Medical Chi Kung Association in Beijing, *it should be clearly stated that medical chi kung does not have the Seven Basic Techniques given in Modern Pranic Healing. The concept of diseased energy was non-existent and is not clear in the mind of the medical chi kung practitioners. Also, they do not use color pranas or colored chi energy for healing.* It is hoped that most of the medical chi kung practitioners will shift from using their own chi energy to external chi energy or pranic energy from the surroundings when doing healing.

MCKS' inquisitive attitude and His avid interest in accumulating more knowledge through study and through experimentation continue to this day.

Mang Dabon

Chapter 3

# MCKS' Meeting with Mang Dabon

In early 1971, when MCKS was about 18 years old, He was introduced to Mang Dabon by His friend, Samuel. Mang Dabon was His first physical spiritual guide. MCKS regularly visited him twice a week for many years.

Mang Dabon was a devout Catholic and he read the Holy Bible regularly. A high Tibetan Lama in his past incarnation, his Spiritual Teacher was a Tibetan Holy Master by the name of Chohan Jig Mei Lingpa, who is a direct disciple of Lord Padmasambhava. Lord Padmasambhava, who was "Born of the Lotus Flower", in his past Egyptian life, was known as the Chief High Priest Nefertem – who was also "Born of the Lotus Flower". In his Indian incarnation, he was known as Avatar Rama. This is why some Arhatic yogis have seen a *blue person* with a bow and arrows during their meditations. Being non-Indian, these Arhatic yogis were unable to identify this Being, until it was explained to them that this Being is actually the Avatar, Lord Rama. Lord Padmasambhava is also known as Lord Mahaguruji Mei Ling.

The name of MCKS' friend has been changed to Samuel in order to protect his privacy.

Great Spiritual Teachers incarnate in different bodies in different countries in order to accelerate the development of the human race. In some instances, they may even establish new religions. It is absurd to think that a Great Spiritual Teacher would incarnate only once and then take a permanent vacation.

It is quite natural for an ordinary soul to incarnate in different bodies, in different cultures and in different religions. This is necessary in order for the soul to have a thorough, complete and balanced development. This is a part of the spiritual evolutionary process.

Mang Dabon was a powerful healer and an expert practitioner of practical Kabbalah. During MCKS' interaction with him, Mang Dabon was able to contact different spiritual beings without the use of magical rituals. He was a very good clairvoyant, the best clairvoyant MCKS has, physically, come across so far.

He was able to consciously leave his body at will and would regularly guide a few selected students in the inner world. Mang Dabon was known as a very powerful healer. There were stories of him being able to raise the dead on two occasions. Stories were also told about him being able to turn off the power of a whole building.

During one of MCKS' visits, an unusual experiment occurred. MCKS' finger was used by Mang Dabon to direct intense pranic energy - to literally burn the cancer of a patient. When the patient came back a few weeks later, his outer skin had also been burned and he showed the burned area to us. MCKS has no idea what happened to the patient. Thirty-three years have passed and MCKS still has not come across a healer who can duplicate the experiment that was done that evening. Mang Dabon was indeed one of the most powerful healers MCKS has ever met.

For many years we discussed many, many esoteric subjects, but strangely, Mang Dabon never taught MCKS or others how to heal. This is probably because Mang Dabon was spiritually advanced. All he had to do was to direct his attention and energy to the patient's affected body part and it would be healed. Because Mang Dabon was spiritually advanced, he did not have to use any healing system. He reminded MCKS of great saints and yogis who could heal just by touching or blessing.

Doing simple healing cannot be compared to the extraordinary healing done by Mang Dabon. This is why MCKS, who was young at that time, assumed that to do this kind of extraordinary healing, you had to be born a gifted healer. This idea was incorrect.

It is because of MCKS' years of interaction with Mang Dabon that His spiritual interest was sustained. Mahaguruji Mei Ling first contacted MCKS through Mang Dabon.

As mentioned earlier in this book, Lord Mahaguruji Mei Ling has been MCKS' Sat Guru since very ancient times, for many incarnations. The term, Sat Guru, means the Primary Permanent Spiritual Teacher. Mang Dabon was sent ahead before the birth of MCKS, in order to take care of Him. The functions of Mang Dabon were:

a. To insure MCKS' continuous interest in spiritual matters.
b. To monitor and protect MCKS at a distance.

c. To help Him in His spiritual practice with or without His conscious awareness.

Mang Dabon also read the past lives of MCKS. He said that in one of MCKS' past lives, MCKS was an English person who authored a certain book or books, thereby hinting that MCKS would be writing books.

Mang Dabon also stated that MCKS would be spreading spiritual teachings. MCKS, who was studying in the university at the time, did not put too much emphasis on the prophecy. He was not aware that He had to write so many books and spread the inner teachings globally. If MCKS had known about His very difficult spiritual mission, He probably would have been overwhelmed by the herculean task and would have avoided completely His destiny.

Lord Mahaguruji Mei Ling and his disciples, being very wise and patient, gently and steadily guided and prepared MCKS to fulfill His dharma, his mission.

Mang Dabon was a kind, loving and helpful person. He was a great yogi, a very good clairvoyant and a powerful healer, an expert practical Kabbalist, and a very good friend. Mang Dabon left his body permanently on 1 November 1981 after a medical surgical operation.

Several months after Mang Dabon left his body, people from different parts of the Philippines and the United States of America went to Cebu City to visit Mang Dabon. They claimed to have recently met and talked with him. They said they had been healed by him. When his children informed the visitors he had left his body, the visitors could not believe it. Mang Dabon had never been in the United States of America, yet when several visitors visited his home, they stated that they had been healed by him in the U.S.A.

To convince the visitors their father had left his body, the children of Mang Dabon took them to the cemetery and showed them where his body was buried.

Chapter 4

# Samuel on Mang Dabon and MCKS



Before I went into the spiritual path, I was no saint. I was just like most young people, smoking, drinking beer and hard liquor, partying and chasing women. These old habits continued to a lesser degree even after I entered the spiritual path.

In 1971, a friend introduced me to a healing center and introduced me to Mang Dabon, known as "Dabon". To my surprise, when I entered, he smiled at me as though he already knew me and beckoned to me to sit beside him. Then, he asked me if I had come to observe or to learn. I told him, "to observe". Smiling and almost laughing, he told me it would be better for me to learn. I found him to be so kind-hearted, that I decided to visit him as often as I could. When I became better acquainted with him, he related some of his personal experiences.

Mang Dabon related to me a personal experience about his Master. During World War II, he and his family were hiding from the Japanese soldiers in the mountains of Leyte. After his work he would read the Bible, but on that day, he was reading a particular passage which he could not understand. He contemplated on it so deeply, that he fell asleep on the floor, with the Bible still in his hand. Suddenly, he was awakened by a being, who nudged his elbow with a foot. When he opened his eyes he saw a big golden being. He looked up. The being was smiling at him and revealed to him the meaning of the passage he had been trying to understand.

At another time, he said that he was awakened again by his Master who told him to go to another island because the invading Japanese soldiers were going to pass by their town. He placed his family in a small boat and proceeded to go to another island. While traveling at sea, there was a sudden strong wind which created big waves. They could no longer guide the boat which was forced toward a rocky ledge. Afraid that the boat would be smashed on the rocks, he prayed to God and invoked the help and blessing of his Spiritual Master. Miraculously, the boat passed through a narrow opening in the rocks, to a safe place inside the island.

He also related to me an event in which he was able to energetically stop the flow of electricity from going into a building - resulting in a power failure in the building.

## Samuel Meets MCKS

I first met MCKS in the middle part of 1971 in the university cafeteria. I was in my third year of study in chemical engineering. MCKS was also studying chemical engineering, but He was in His first year.

I vividly remember the occasion. I was reading a book on yoga. I glanced up to rest my eyes and saw a scholarly young student approaching me. He was wearing a bright green t-shirt and unpolished leather shoes without socks. As He came closer, He asked me about my esoteric interests other than yoga. I answered that so far, I had read only books on yoga, but that I wanted to learn about other esoteric sciences. I told MCKS that I had six books on yoga and offered to lend Him one. He answered, "Why not?" Then, He said that He would also lend me some of His books. I was so eager to know about His books and asked Him, "When can we exchange books?" He told me we could go to His house at about the same time next week.

On the way to His house the following week, He led me through a short cut, through some narrow streets. I thought that He lived in one of those small, poor houses, because He was modestly clothed and was so unassuming in His manner. But to my surprise, we ended up at a big building which was His residence. I was even more startled to see that He had a library of many esoteric books. I was so glad that He befriended me. This started the beginning of my education in the esoteric sciences. He lent me books on Edgar Cayce, on the Kabbalah, on the Golden Dawn, books by George Gurdieff, by Arthur Edward Powell, Rosicrucian books, Astara books and others. He also lent me many Theosophical books including the *Secret Doctrine* by Madame Blavatsky.

In 1971, I invited MCKS to visit a friend of mine, who was a practicing Kabbalist, Mang Dabon. We went to visit Mang Dabon in his healing center in Pasil, a ghetto in Cebu City. When we entered the healing center, he was quite busy healing a patient. Suddenly, he turned his head and acknowledged our presence as though he knew we were coming. Then, he called to me and whispered in my ear that my friend is a practitioner of the inner sciences. He asked MCKS to come nearer and I introduced them.

Mang Dabon was a man for the common people. His patients were mostly poor people. Most rich people would not think of going into a dangerous ghetto for healing.

We had a lively conversation regarding healing and the manipulation of energies. On the third visit to the healing center of Mang Dabon, an interesting event happened. I noticed that a fly was flying around, disturbing our conversation. MCKS asked, "Would you like to see a demonstration of the manipulation of energy?" He then pointed His finger at the fly and the fly got stuck on the floor. I noticed it stayed there for a while. I tried to shoo it off, but it would not fly away, so I instinctively tried to step on the fly but MCKS gestured to me not to do it. I also noticed that Mang Dabon nodded his head with approval, signifying that MCKS was already relatively advanced in His practice.

On another occasion, MCKS did an experiment by energizing my forehead area with His right index finger, projecting a beam of energy into my forehead. I felt my forehead become warm. After a few minutes, I felt something like a cork screw boring into my head. This energy seemed to have activated my clairvoyance faculty because after that, I could spontaneously see Spirit Beings more clearly and frequently. The accelerated development of my clairvoyant faculty was an unexpected benefit.

Then we did another experiment. I asked MCKS if I put on an energy shield, whether I would still feel it if He projects energy to me. He said yes, so I shielded myself. He then projected a bolt of energy. It bounced off. So MCKS increased the intensity of the projected energy by several times. When it hit me, I had to move my right foot behind me in order to prevent my body from falling backward. This stronger energy bolt penetrated my energy shield and I felt a tearing sensation in my chest.

After the experiment, I returned home a bit dizzy. Three days after this energy experiment, I noticed a lump in my throat. When I spat it out, it was blood. So I went to another well respected healer, Mang Nenet, and asked him to clairvoyantly check to see what was wrong with me. He responded that there was a hole in the inner aura the size of his little finger. He did healing on me but could not close the hole in my energy body. Then, he said I should go back to the person who had done this and ask that person to heal me. This accident occurred in about 1972, but I did not tell MCKS about it. Because I was hard headed and thought I could heal myself, I did not ask MCKS to heal me until 2003. After His healing, the pain vanished instantly and I have had no reoccurrence of the pain since.

All of these three experiments were done in 1971 and 1972 when MCKS was only about 19 years old.

A few weeks later, there was another interesting event. Mang Dabon was healing a middle aged patient who had stomach cancer. Mang Dabon took the right hand of MCKS and pointed MCKS' finger at the patient. Mang Dabon projected energy through the finger of MCKS. The patient was visibly affected. He appeared to be uneasy, because he felt uncomfortable and was trying to control his movements. After a few minutes, the healing session ended. The patient was instructed to come back. Several weeks later, he showed the previously treated area. We saw that even the outer skin on the abdominal area had been visibly burned.

On another occasion, I went to Mang Dabon's healing center quite early, before Mang Dabon arrived. I saw some patients and asked one of them if he would mind my healing him. I made several hand passes over his shoulder which the patient claimed was aching. Then, Mang Dabon arrived. He shook his head in disapproval. He told me that I was doing it all wrong and took over. He healed the patient for a few minutes after which the patient told Mang Dabon the pain was completely gone.

Another interesting event happened during one of my visits. Mang Dabon touched my left shoulder and his clairvoyance was transferred to me. The patient's body became transparent and I was able to see the internal organs of the patient. I could see what was wrong because some of the organs looked dark. According to MCKS, this is called *guided transferred clairvoyance.*

On another occasion, Mang Dabon told me about reviving the dead. A man fell from a coconut tree and died. The man's friend called for Mang Dabon because he was known to be a good healer. By the time Mang Dabon arrived at the location, the man had been dead for about one hour. Mang Dabon did healing and the man was miraculously revived.

Another interesting story Mang Dabon related to me was about his businessman friend who had lost a lot of money. He came to Mang Dabon for help. Mang Dabon told him to buy cocoa beans. He told his friend to buy as much as he could, because in three months' time the price of the beans would increase substantially. His friend rented a very large warehouse and filled it with cocoa beans. Exactly three months later, the price increased so much that the businessman became very rich. He tried to give Mang Dabon a new car as a token of appreciation, but Mang Dabon did not accept the gift. Mang Dabon was a righteous man who was not influenced by money.

Noticing my skepticism about his stories and experiences, he shifted the topic to astral travel. He asked how much I had progressed. I told him that I was only able to do astral travel for a few minutes then, I would lose consciousness. He said, "Then I will teach you about astral travel". I was wondering why he did not give me any verbal instructions. That evening, Mang Dabon appeared at the foot of my bed and my physical body became drowsy. At the moment of falling asleep, Mang Dabon took my right hand and jerked my consciousness out of my physical body. While fully aware, he brought me to different realms of the astral world. In one realm, a certain category of disincarnate souls are contained - much like a community. These souls of varying degrees of spiritual maturity are confined within different realms. This happened almost every night for about six months.

## Samuel's First Spiritual Experience

During the later part of my training with Mang Dabon, while I was meditating, in my inner vision, I saw a black spot about the size of a small button. The black spot felt like a whirlpool. It felt like I was being sucked into it. I was afraid. I materialized a "post" beside me and clung to it desperately so that I would not be sucked into the black hole. At that moment, I got out of my meditation.

## Samuel's Second Spiritual Experience

The second time, the experience was not so forceful. This time it was as if the black spot was inviting me inside. So I dove into it much like jumping into a swimming pool. I found myself spiritually transported into a blue world. The Spiritual Guide looked very, very big, and was attired like a Tibetan monk, only dressed in blue. He was totally blue in a blue world. And what a drab world it was. No other colors, not even green or red.

The Spiritual Guide's face could not be seen because it was radiating with so much light. I was not alone. We were six students on a "flying blue carpet". The Spiritual Guide instructed us to stay within the confines of this blue flying carpet.

In the blue world, our Guide showed us blue persons performing rituals, performing mudras or hand gestures, as well as practicing meditation. We exited the blue world through a white sphere and my physical body woke up.

## Samuel's Third Spiritual Experience

The third time, I performed certain mudras and went into meditation. When I entered the black spot, I experienced profound bliss.

## Samuel's Fourth Spiritual Experience

The fourth time I entered the blue world, I found myself in a dark void. It was such a dark void, much like a moonless night. I heard a voice asking me what I wanted to do. I knelt down and prayed. As I started to say, "Our Father", I, the soul, exploded as brilliant light and expanded. I was expanding in the inner universe. I experienced that I, the soul, was everywhere simultaneously. I was simply pure consciousness - without a body or form. The *divine ecstasy* was so intense, that my body woke up and was gasping for breath.

These spiritual experiences occurred during the six month period when Mang Dabon was guiding me in the inner world. The first spiritual experience occurred on the fourth month. The second spiritual experience occurred four days after the first one. The third spiritual experience occurred after the fifth month. The fourth experience happened on the last day of the sixth month. After that, I was not able to recapture such wonderful, intense spiritual experiences.

I do not regret being unable to experience again the *divine oneness* and *divine ecstasy,* since other yogis may meditate for a lifetime and never experience a portion of what I have experienced. I am very grateful for the divine blessings I have received.

In 2004, I narrated the experience of the black spot to MCKS. He explained to me that it was not really a black spot, but the *blue pearl* or the mental permanent seed. This blue pearl is the "gateway to the higher world", the "gateway to heaven". In the Indian tradition, the crown chakra is called the "gateway to God", and the blue pearl is located at the root of the crown chakra. This is why the Lord Jesus said, "Heaven is not here, there or anywhere. It is within you". (Luke 17:21)

On 16 September 2005, when I was narrating my experiences to MCKS about the flying carpet, He explained to me that the blue flying carpet is actually a thought form created by the Spiritual Teacher to confine the students within a certain space for their own protection. Otherwise, the students would tend to travel into different parts of the inner world and it would be difficult for the Spiritual Guide to monitor, guard and protect them.

I realized, after 34 years, that the Spiritual Guide was actually Mang Dabon. MCKS clarified and explained to me these four spiritual experiences.

MCKS explained to me that the reasons why I did not recognize Mang Dabon as the Spiritual Guide was because:

1. The Guide was much bigger and looked so different from the physical body of Mang Dabon.

2. I could not see the face because it was so radiant with light and was not recognizable.

3. I did not recognize Mang Dabon as the Tibetan Master, because I identified Mang Dabon as the physical body.

## Experience with the Law of Karma

In around 1994, my fiancé of 8 years was very angry with me and pointed a gun at my head. She pulled the trigger. Miraculously, the gun did not fire! A few days later, I sensed something bad might happen to her. I called her by telephone and asked her to apologize. She was still very angry and said, "The next time I will make sure the gun will fire!" After about 3 weeks, she was in a fatal bus accident. When I saw her body, there was a hole in her head and a bolt was extracted from that hole.

Evidently, during the accident, a bolt was dislodged from the bus and flew into her head - in the exact spot where she was pointing the gun at my head.

Because of my training with Mang Dabon, I was able to visit her in the inner world. I tried to bring her out of that realm. To reach her, it was necessary to pass an astral bridge. When my left astral foot touched the edge of the astral bridge, my astral body was catapulted across, to the other side of the bridge. My fiancé was sucked back into her realm. The spiritual guardian of the realm told me not to return. After several years, I met Mang Dabon in the inner world (he left his body in 1981). Through his intercession, I was allowed to see my former girlfriend, but only within her realm.

Mang Nenet

Mang Mike

Chapter 5

# MCKS' Meeting with Mang Nenet and Mang Mike



## MCKS' Meeting with Mang Nenet

In about 1972, Samuel introduced MCKS to Mang Nenet. The father of Mang Nenet was a recognized poet, worked as secretary for two governors of Cebu, and established the first Theosophical Society in the Philippines in Cebu City.

According to stories, the spiritual teacher of Mang Nenet was his father, whose guru was an Indian swami. Whether or not he met his Indian swami guru physically, it was not clarified. The father of Mang Nenet left his body when Mang Nenet was still a child.

Mang Nenet studied law and became a lawyer. He was a devout Catholic and he prayed the rosary regularly. The form of healing that he used was *oracion* or healing by prayer in Latin. He was also a clairvoyant and was in telepathic contact with his father and some spiritual teachers.

From a list of esoteric books, Mang Nenet taught and lectured to his disciples regularly. These lectures lasted for several years. He placed a lot of emphasis on learning, on the accumulation of esoteric information, and on the mental development of his students.

Mang Nenet was an expert in making talismans. There was a case of a person who was usually not feeling well, and he thought that he was being energetically attacked. Mang Nenet gave him a protective amulet. After that, his health problems disappeared.

One day, that person felt a severe back pain and could hardly move for three days. Later, somebody informed him that Mang Nenet left his body permanently. It seems that when Mang Nenet passed away, the amulet lost its power.

Mang Nenet was a very kind and good person who cared a lot about his students and nurtured them for many years. Mang Nenet left his body on 29 November 1999.

## MCKS' Meeting with Mang Mike

Mang Mike was introduced to MCKS by Samuel in about 1975. MCKS visited Mang Mike a few times in Cebu City prior to Mang Mike's departure for Iran to work as a master baker. He was a kind and very accommodating person. He was a gentle soul, full of love for others and a good clairvoyant.

Mang Mike was from a super rich family. His sisters were sent abroad to study, in Spain. Mang Mike's mother forced him to study engineering, against his will. He was not good in mathematics and science so he shifted his study to liberal arts. He graduated with a Bachelor of Liberal Arts degree, with honors. His major study was in English. His parents and family were very happy with him. Mang Mike became a good concert pianist and was also a wonderful singer. He was compared to the famous Mario Lanza.

Unfortunately, most of his brothers and sisters were not interested in the family business. When his parents died, their family lost almost everything. This crisis was actually a great blessing in disguise for Mang Mike, as it *drove him to search for spiritual truth. It drove him into the spiritual path.* Mang Mike was also very generous and supportive of his immediate family.

Mang Mike spent many years spreading the Baha'i teachings. In spite of being overweight, he walked into the mountains to teach the Baha'i faith. He was indeed a good evangelist. He also taught the Baha'i faith in the national penitentiary. The conditions there were rather dangerous, yet he persisted in teaching the Baha'i faith. All of these qualities are very praiseworthy.

In about 1981, Mang Mike was paralyzed due to a stroke. He was hospitalized, given proper medication and physical therapy while in the hospital and after being discharged from the hospital.

Later, MCKS visited him in his house in Cebu City where he was still bedridden and unable to walk. MCKS gave him two or three healing treatments using divine energy. After that, Mang Mike recovered rapidly and was able to walk and travel. In about August of that year, Mang Mike traveled from Cebu City to Cubao, Quezon City, where he stayed with his sister.

Both Mang Nenet and Mang Mike later played important roles in Pranic Healing and Arhatic Yoga. Mang Dabon also played a very important role in the inner world through guided transferred clairvoyancy during the experiments and provided assistance in healing.

The name of Mang Mike's Spiritual Teacher was Holy Master Gemaliel.

Mang Mike left his body permanently on 15 February 2003.

Chapter 6

# Samuel on Mang Nenet and Mang Mike



## Samuel Meets Mang Nenet

In the later part of 1971, I was invited to attend a meeting of an esoteric group of eight people where I met Mang Nenet, known as "Nenet", and Mang Mike, known as "Mike".

Mang Nenet was a clairvoyant. He healed by using prayer. Mang Nenet was the lecturer that morning and he discussed the different paths and trials an aspirant would undergo in his quest for enlightenment. As I listened to him, other members of the group were trying to read my aura. After Mang Nenet's lecture, they all agreed I would be welcome to visit them at anytime. They said they would gladly help me with my desire to learn more about the inner world.

According to Mang Nenet, when he was young, he was very human. Like many young people, he smoked, drank and chased after women. Later in his life, his Spiritual Teacher (without a physical body) contacted him and told him to give up these vices in order to progress on the spiritual path.

The purpose of this narrative is to show that if Mang Nenet could spiritually transform himself, then it is also possible for ordinary people to give up their vices and to spiritually progress.

After I became more acquainted with Mang Nenet, I visited him regularly. On one occasion, he made an amulet for me to wear. He told me that this would accelerate my spiritual evolution. The amulet made me very uncomfortable, but after a few days I managed to adjust to it. Not long after, on several occasions, I could spontaneously hear people's thoughts, which sounded as though they were from inside an earthen jar.

Some months later, he gave me another amulet which he said would stop guns from firing if someone tried to shoot me.

Many years later, I was able to experience the effectivity of the amulet. A band of paramilitary men fired at me but their weapons did not fire. They had to eject the bullets inside the barrel and reload the magazine of the automatic rifles. When they tried to fire a second time, again their guns simply did not fire. Before they could reload a third time, their leader, who recognized me as an engineer, told them to stop. I was very thankful to God that I was still alive; and thankful to Mang Nenet that he had foreseen the need for this protection. Thankful, too, that he had given me this special type of amulet, otherwise, my body would have been completely riddled with bullet holes.

Sometime in the later part of 1972, I was in the house of MCKS. He asked me if I knew any other clairvoyants living in Cebu City. I told Him, "Yes, I know a man by the name of Mang Nenet". MCKS asked if I could call him and make an appointment to visit him. One week later, we went to his house which served as his ashram. After introducing MCKS to Mang Nenet, I could see from his face that he was very pleased to have made MCKS' acquaintance. From that moment on, MCKS would go to Mang Nenet's place whenever time would permit.

My meetings with Mang Nenet were very limited. He had to attend to his business aside from teaching. Therefore, our meetings were either early in the morning or in the evening because otherwise, he would have just a little time to attend to his disciples.

Mang Nenet was quite secretive. He told me many stories about his father, but nothing about himself. He told me that if his father wanted to teleport himself to another place, he would secure a picture of the place and teleport himself through the picture, thereby reaching the place that he wanted.

On another occasion, the father of Mang Nenet was by the seashore where heavy rain was about to pour. The salt makers were trying to gather the salt they had made throughout the day, but it seemed that they could not gather it fast enough before the downpour. Seeing this, the father of Mang Nenet raised his hands as though he was about to lift something. Although the clouds were very dark and the rain had started, there was no rain on the salt fields. After the salt makers had stored the harvested salt into their huts, he put his hands down, and then the rain began to pour.

One day, we went to the house of Mang Nenet in the late afternoon to practice a meditation for the Wesak Festival. He told me to meditate alone in the balcony because the living room was reserved for his disciples only. However, he allowed MCKS to remain in the living room to meditate with the group.

After about an hour, the group asked me to join them in the living room. They were discussing what they had seen clairvoyantly during the Wesak Festival.

MCKS reported that, "while floating in front of the very large body of the Lord Buddha during the Wesak, He felt like a small mosquito floating. It seemed that there were arrows radiating out of the body of the Lord Buddha". Later, MCKS realized that these "arrows" coming out of the Lord Buddha's body were actually rays of light.

Mang Nenet told MCKS that He had described it correctly. He said he had also projected himself into the Wesak Festival. Mang Nenet concurred that what MCKS had seen was the same as that which he had observed.

According to Mang Nenet, the arrows are actually blessings from the Lord Buddha to the world. These *blessings* or *light* radiating from the Lord Buddha were interpreted by the brain of MCKS as arrows. This is one of the possible problems that may be encountered by a disciple - the partial distortion of inner experiences by the physical brain.

## Samuel's First Meeting with Mang Mike

The first time I met Mang Mike was through Maning in 1971. He introduced me to a group of interesting people which included Mang Nenet and Mang Mike.

During my interaction with Mang Mike in Cebu, he did not do healing as he was a practicing clairvoyant reader who gave psychic readings.

In the later part of 1971, an interesting event occurred during an afternoon at Mang Mike's residence and bakery store. I saw him go into his bedroom. Later, I also went into the room but I could not find him. I noticed that there were subdued sparks of light in the room. I came out of the room, sat outside and continued my conversation with two of his bakers. I told the bakers that it would have been impossible for Mang Mike to leave the room without us noticing him because we were sitting just outside the door. They all agreed that it would have been impossible for him to leave the room unnoticed.

Later, during our lively conversation, Mang Mike shouted from inside the room, "Hey, you guys are very noisy". When I went into his room, I was surprised to see him and asked him where he had gone. He replied that he had been teleported by his Master to a room in a hotel in Argentina, to attend a meeting with his Master and the rest of his Master's disciples. He clarified that he did not teleport himself, but that he was teleported through the power of his Teacher.

In about 1975, I consulted Mang Mike about my progress in meditation practice. He asked me to meditate regularly and to come and consult with him every three days.

Chapter 7

# Raphy on Uncle Mike and MCKS

In 1970, my family lived together with four other families, in one big family house in Cebu City. I remember my Uncle Mike as being a heavy smoker, smoking one ream or carton of cigarettes per day. He was constantly reading thick books, even while he was having a conversation with me.

I spent lots of time with him. I would even fall asleep beside him as he would read me stories. He would frequently send me to buy ice cream - ice cream in the morning, in the afternoon and in the evening. Our favorite flavors were mango and ube*.

He also disciplined all of his nephews and nieces and was feared by most of us. He was very generous and he helped pay for our school tuition, sending most of us to school.

Also, as I remember, he did some mathematical computations for the lottery. While doing that, he was almost always smoking. His room was between the sala (living room) and the kitchen, near the refrigerator.

* purple yam

I also remember, that about once per month, there were lots of people gathering in the house. He would talk to them, much like holding a seminar. During weekends, I would always go out and watch movies with him and some of my cousins.

Uncle Mike, his three brothers, two sisters and friends played mahjong almost every night, especially on Friday and Saturday night.

In the late 1970's or early 80's, as soon as he received his salary, he would usually ask me to pay for the items he got from the grocery store on credit. Sometimes, he would pay for the food for everyone in the house to help his sister with the household expenses.

If we asked him to buy something for us or even if we asked him for cash, as long as we explained the purpose, he would gladly comply. We were usually asking for money for food. Most of the time, he would spend for the snacks.

He was working in Foodarama Bakeshop as the chief baker and manager. It was a bakeshop connected to a large grocery store. I usually went there in the afternoon, after coming home from school. He would ask me to taste the bread and give me fresh baked bread. He also gave me some bread to take home to the entire family.

In September of 1980, my family and I moved to Manila. After that time, I lost contact with him until 1981 when I heard that he had a stroke. Since I was only about 13 years old and was in my first year of high school, I was unable to return to Cebu City to see him.

My uncle underwent physical therapy and eventually was able to walk and recover some of his reflexes. He reduced his weight dramatically.

In the same year, Mommy Inday (my aunt) told me that Uncle Mike was coming to Manila to help with the bakeshop she opened. My aunt and Uncle Mike began managing the bakeshop. From that time on, I saw them regularly.

About 1982, my aunt had a slight stroke and she returned to Cebu City. I was left in Metro Manila and helped Uncle Mike to sell bread. My task was to sell bread in school, in the cafeteria, and to some of my classmates. I was able to earn about 20 to 25 centavos per piece. This helped me to pay for my school tuition.

Uncle Mike taught me how to convince my classmates to buy the ensaymada* bread even though it was more expensive. He told me to make an arrangement with the canteen to lend me a case of soft drink, have the case brought to the third floor so that my classmates would not have to go downstairs to buy soft drinks. As a result, most of my classmates bought from me and I was able to sell all of the bread. I had lots of money.

Those classmates who did not pay, paid me the next day so, I would give the bread in advance. There was one instance, when a classmate, who was a bully, would not pay for the bread so I ended up paying for it. I told my uncle that there was a difference in the cash intake because some of my classmates were not able to pay. The remittance was short. He then taught me how to collect more effectively.

* soft sugar sprinkled butter bread

The first time I saw MCKS was during the school semester break in 1982. He visited Uncle Mike who stayed in the bakeshop during the afternoons. MCKS would buy bread and soft drinks from the bakery for snacks for all of us.

MCKS and my uncle usually sat at a table in front of the bakery, having snacks and talking. Almost everyday, MCKS went to the bakeshop to visit him. Later, Uncle Mike moved to Harvard Street, the next street across from the bakery, and managed the bakery from his home.

From 1982 until about 1985 (my first year in the university) MCKS began visiting my uncle almost everyday. I went to school at night and took care of my uncle in the morning and afternoon. Everyday, from 1 p.m. to 6 p.m., I would see my uncle and MCKS talking and doing some experiments.

Everyday, when I went to school at 6 p.m., MCKS would drive me to school. I have many memories of MCKS with my uncle; and sometimes I was also the subject for their experiments. For example, one time, MCKS made a gesture of energizing a big capsule, and then He asked me to take it. He then asked my uncle to observe the effect while I sat in between them. These experiments occurred in the apartment in Harvard Street.

Another experiment involved a lighted candle. Asking my uncle to clairvoyantly observe the effect, MCKS dropped the hot wax on my hand. Then, He projected energy and asked me if I felt any pain. Of course, it was painful at first, but eventually, I did not feel any pain. Although I saw the skin of my hand turn red, the pain was gone.

During the monthly Full Moon Meditation, MCKS was usually around.

Every time MCKS went to see my uncle, He would send me to buy a large pizza or big Chinese buns. We were always happy when He was with us, because there were always snacks for everybody. Whenever MCKS was around, everyone else would go upstairs to leave the two of them in the sala (living room) to practice meditations and do experiments. This happened everyday.

Sometimes we went up at about 12 noon or 1 p.m. and came down at about 6 p.m. MCKS would still be there meditating with Uncle Mike, who would be clairvoyantly monitoring His meditation. This means MCKS had been meditating for about 5 hours.

In about 1986, MCKS asked me to start reading computer print-outs of the Pranic Healing book, to see if I could understand what had been written. When I was unable to understand something, He would simplify the words using the simplest terms possible. MCKS mentioned that there was no point in writing a book if it cannot be understood by the common people. In 1987, MCKS published his first book and founded the Institute for Inner Studies, Incorporated.

MCKS did more experiments. Once, at the start of the Meditation on Twin Hearts, He gave me shaktipat or spiritual empowerment on my back. He asked me to sit on a stool facing east. Then, He asked me to relax every muscle in my body. He asked me to relax my shoulders, my eyebrows, my hands, my cheeks, my feet, my legs - so that every part was very relaxed. Then suddenly, he hit me on the back between my shoulder blades. I felt helplessly propelled forward. As I slowly recovered, my body was aching everywhere, where it hit the floor. Then He asked me, "Raphy, are you all right?" I responded, "Yes", and pretended that nothing felt painful. I did not know if He was angry with me or what had happened because I was so totally relaxed. I was defenseless, unable to even hold onto the chair or anything.

Much earlier, MCKS did similar experiments with my Uncle Mike. He gave him shaktipat, by gently hitting him on the upper back.

There were also some experiments regarding the Golden Body, but I cannot relate them, as per MCKS' instructions.

In 1987, from Cubao, my uncle moved to Mei Ling Healing Center in Kamuning. MCKS provided the Mei Ling Healing Center for my Uncle Mike. At this time, I was not living with my uncle. However, I regularly visited my uncle at this center where he and MCKS spent most of their time doing healing. Also, during this time, MCKS began holding regular Pranic Healing seminars on Saturdays and Sundays.

In late 1988, my uncle moved to Project 8 in Quezon City. Then, he moved again in late 1989, this time to Maria Clara Street. Again, MCKS provided this house for my uncle and once again, I lived with my uncle. MCKS continued visiting my uncle, and they continued doing experiments together, with my uncle clairvoyantly monitoring them. Full Moon Meditations also continued on a regular monthly basis.

In about 1994, my uncle and I moved to a house on Samat Street which was provided by MCKS. We had lots of activities especially during each full moon evening.

When we lived in the house on Samat Street, I had to bring my uncle to the hospital so many times. He had difficulty breathing, he had several mild strokes, and he had internal bleeding. Once when he was sitting on the toilet, his helper came to me. He said that there was something wrong with my uncle's face. I saw the common signs, that he was having a stroke. I asked the helper to assist me in lifting him to the bed. It was a scary time because I thought he was going to pass away. We rushed him to the Philippine Heart Center, but his heart was strong and he survived. Again, MCKS provided money for everything, paying for his hospital bills and all expenses.

The following year, he had another attack, this time, with difficulty in breathing. I asked my wife to go with me in the ambulance. While driving to the hospital, the ambulance hit another car. Suddenly, Uncle Mike regained consciousness due to the shake up and we were able to reach the hospital. On this occasion, he instructed me to change some of his personal accounts into joint accounts with me. He wanted to avoid problems when he passed away. He said I had always been there to take care of him and that now, he would be there to take care of me.

Whenever I went to Baguio City, he would always look for me and asked when I would return home. At that time, he knew he would last for only a few more years and he was preparing for it.

Most of this time, MCKS was very busy spreading the teachings in other countries, but when He would eventually return home to the Philippines, He would regularly visit Uncle Mike. MCKS and my Uncle Mike were very good friends. MCKS was always very kind, helpful and generous to Uncle Mike and his immediate family.

In about 2001, we moved to a larger house in Visayas Street which was again provided by MCKS.

While MCKS was in India teaching, my Uncle Mike left his body permanently on 15 February 2003.

Chapter 8

# Spiritual Immunization

When MCKS was young, He lived in a very sheltered, protected environment. In about 1976, He moved to Makati City, Metro Manila, to do a graduate study in business management. His classmates were not only from the Philippines, but were also from the United States of America, the United Kingdom, and other countries.

In that school, He was partially introduced to night life and women. It was educational and interesting. MCKS was definitely not a monk and did not want to be one. He just wanted to be a good person.

Later, He went into business and was further exposed to the real world, which was very different from His previously sheltered life. His experiences were sometimes interesting and sometimes unpleasant. All of this is a part of life and was a part of the maturing process of the soul.

This immersion in a pool of muddy water is a necessary process for one's spiritual development, whether in this incarnation or in the past incarnations. When a person has always been living in a medically sterile environment, the body will not survive when exposed to the outside world because it does not have a strong, experienced immune defense system to handle the disease causing microbes in the real world.

Likewise, a disciple who has been living in a spiritually sanitized and protected environment will succumb to vices because the soul does not have sufficient experience nor the inner strength to overcome the actual conditions in the real world.

It took MCKS effort and time to overcome certain weaknesses.

One of the common problems experienced by disciples is unregulated excessive sexual activities. This could be due to a puritanical sexual upbringing.

A puritanical sexual attitude prevents the sex energy from naturally flowing up to the upper chakras. This incorrect sexual attitude causes the sex energy to be stuck in the sex chakra, which strongly activates the sexual desire, making it obsessive and compulsive.

Unregulated excessive sexual activities could also be caused by hedonistic attitudes about sex. In this case, the sexual urge is unregulated and uncontrolled. The sex energy is just simply wasted.

Both puritanical and hedonistic attitudes toward sex lead to sexual enslavement manifesting as uncontrolled excessive sexual activities. The proper approach is the *middle path.*

The proper attitude is to consider sex as natural. What is required is the *regulation of sexual energy and transforming* it into:

1. Heart energy manifesting as love, compassion, kindness, and intimacy;

2. Throat energy manifesting as greater and higher intelligence and creativity;
3. Crown energy manifesting as spiritual energy, and greater connectedness and oneness with the Higher Soul.

It is not advisable for spiritually young disciples to practice sexual celibacy, unless he or she has been living a sexually hedonistic lifestyle in this incarnation or in previous incarnations. In this case, temporary sexual celibacy is needed in order to develop a certain degree of self control. Otherwise, the disciple will not be able to overcome the sexual addiction.

A disciple with sexual problems must have proper psychological counseling and must undergo Pranic Psychotherapy treatments.

If required by custom, sexual celibacy may be practiced for a certain period of time. Also, if required by the rules of the religious order, sexual celibacy may be practiced. But, the practice of sexual celibacy should be accompanied by the regular practice of transforming sexual energies into higher energies.

For senior spiritual disciples, the practice of conserving sexual energy will occur naturally as they mature.

The soul is sexless and a person is not the body. It is natural for one soul to love another soul regardless of the gender of the physical body. Sexual preference does not reflect on the spiritual development of the soul.

A disciple also has to overcome other weaknesses, such as addiction to smoking, alcoholic drinks and/or addictive drugs. All of these must be avoided. A disciple with these problems should seek external assistance.

Addiction to gambling is also very dangerous and must be avoided. This is just sheer foolishness.

A disciple with proper spiritual training is usually much more intelligent than the common people. Therefore, they may tend to develop pride, gloating and enviousness. This may also manifest as being excessively critical towards others. All of these weaknesses must be eliminated.

A spiritual disciple may also be exposed to the opportunity of earning lots of money. Earning lots of money is good. To be wealthy is good. Wealth must preferably be in the hands of spiritually developed people with goodwill and the will to do good. But if the spiritual disciple loses his self-control, this may manifest as greed, ruthlessness, and deception. All of these must also be eliminated. Excessive, unregulated desire for money may also divert the spiritual disciple from his spiritual practice. This must be avoided.

A spiritual disciple, having a higher standard than others, may tend to develop impatience, anger, intolerance and excessive criticism toward others. All of these must be overcome and eliminated.

A disciple may also be addicted to success and tend to overwork. This will lead to poor health and serious ailments if not, the early termination of the physical body. All of these must be avoided.

A spiritual disciple, being internally good and kind, may project these qualities to others who are not mature and not kind. This may lead to gullibility and being easily fooled by others. A disciple must be on guard against this tendency.

A disciple is usually kind and generous to most people. Unfortunately, there are some who will respond with ingratitude, with betrayal and treachery and even with maliciousness. Many disciples will respond with anger, hatred, bitterness, inner pain and sometimes even with vengeance. All of these must be gradually overcome. A disciple must learn to be patient, to understand, to be tolerant, to be compassionate, to internally forgive and to bless. Although the disciple has internally forgiven the offending person(s), it is still necessary, in some instances, to take actions that may be, to a certain extent severe, in order for the person to learn his lesson and not commit the same serious mistake again. It is also necessary to protect possible future victims.

*A disciple must develop discernment or intelligent evaluation. Without discernment, a disciple can easily be influenced and manipulated by others. Therefore, his trustworthiness and loyalty cannot be guaranteed. A disciple with no discernment may even betray and attack his own spiritual guru and his organization. The Virtue of Discernment or Intelligent Evaluation must be developed in all disciples.*

Inner Purification or Character Building is extremely important. Without thorough continuous Character Building, a disciple will spiritually fall. This is exactly what happened to some of MCKS' disciples. They did not focus enough on Character Building and spiritually fell because of pride, self delusion, arrogance, greed and dishonesty.

*A disciple with serious character flaws must not be embarrassed to seek external assistance and request for Pranic Psychotherapy.*

The incarnated soul is likened to a lotus flower. It is rooted in muddy water. The lotus bud is also in the muddy water. Eventually, the bud will rise out of the muddy water and blooms towards the sky and the sun.

The muddy water symbolizes earthly existence. The bud symbolizes the 12th chakra where the incarnated soul is anchored. Eventually, the soul will achieve illumination and the 12th chakra will bloom into a fiery golden lotus flower.

The sun symbolizes God or the Supreme Being - the soul reaches out towards God, and achieves greater connectedness and oneness with God.

The earth symbolizes excessive materialism and greed. The water symbolizes enslavement by unregulated desires and chaotic emotions. Through the gentle guidance of the teachings from the Great Spiritual Teachers of different religions and the constant steering by the Law of Karma, which manifests as painful and pleasant experiences, the soul inevitably learns the lessons, gains inner strength and spiritually evolves until it achieves illumination, oneness with the Higher Soul, oneness with the Divine Spark and greater oneness with God.

This is the meaning of the story about Lord Buddha. When the Lord Buddha achieved his great enlightenment, he was not sure whether the masses would understand his profound teachings. He had a vision of many lotus buds about to rise up and bloom. All that they needed were his priceless teachings.

As stated earlier, the lotus bud symbolizes the 12th chakra or the Pentecostal fire in the Christian tradition. When the soul achieves illumination, the 12th chakra literally blooms and turns into a fiery golden lotus flower.

According to Buddhist tradition, the Lord Buddha was able to produce 10 great disciples, 18 senior arhats, 1,200 arhats. The 18 senior arhats, in turn, produced 16,000 arhats. These arhats are actually the lotus buds that rose out of the muddy water and bloomed, achieving illumination. The blooming of the lotus buds is actually the blossoming of the souls.

May all the readers rise out of the muddy water and bloom into fiery golden lotus flowers. May all be blessed by the Supreme God. May all be blessed by the great, great ones, and by all the great Spiritual Teachers of all religions. Blessings be to All. So be it!

Note: An arhat in the inner tradition is one who has achieved a substantial degree of illumination and oneness with the Higher Soul. Traditionally, arhat means saint. An Arhatic yogi is one who practices Arhatic Yoga and is striving to become a baby arhat.

Chapter 9

# MCKS' Spiritual Thesis



When a disciple reaches a certain level of spiritual development, he has to have a spiritual thesis or spiritual project. In ancient times, the spiritual thesis or project had a great impact within the country or even within the region. Due to the advanced technology of modern times, this spiritual thesis or project has, in many instances, global beneficial impact.

MCKS' Spiritual Thesis is Spiritual Technology or Applied Inner Sciences especially in the areas of:

1. Pranic Healing
2. Arhatic Yoga - Advanced spiritual practices
3. Pranic Feng Shui
4. Kriyashakti, the Science and Art of Becoming Prosperous and Successful using Inner Sciences,

5. Higher Clairvoyancy, and
6. Other spiritual technologies.

His thesis advisor is His Sat Guru, Lord Mahaguruji Mei Ling assisted by his senior disciples especially Chohan Jig Mei Lingpa and also Mang Dabon. The role of Mang Nenet and Mang Mike was to clairvoyantly observe through guided transferred higher clairvoyancy by Chohan Jig Mei Lingpa or Mang Dabon. Other senior disciples also helped.

## The Divine Plan

To understand the nature of MCKS' Spiritual Thesis, it is necessary to have a small glimpse of the Divine Plan of the Planetary Logos or Planetary Parabrahman. This small glimpse of the Divine Plan was hinted by the Holy Master D. K. through his disciple, Alice Bailey, in his book, *Initiation, Human and Solar*. It was prophesized that in the later part of the 20th century, healing using pranic energy would be popularized globally. These are not the exact words of Alice Bailey, but they contain the essence of the message.

## Fulfillment of The Divine Plan

To fulfill this portion of the Divine Plan, many disciples were sent to incarnate on the planet, Earth. The Russian disciples called their healing art as Bioenergy Healing. The Chinese disciples called their healing art, medical chi kung. The Japanese disciples called their healing art as Mahikari and Reiki. *MCKS called this science and art of healing, Pranic Healing.* Other disciples called their healing art as: Psychic Healing, Faith Healing, Charismatic Healing, Magnetic Healing, Therapeutic Touch, and others. Most of the disciples are not physically aware that they are disciples and that their mission in this incarnation is to propagate the art of healing.

## Intuitive Intelligence

To understand the development of Modern Pranic Healing, it is necessary to understand certain important concepts:

1. Intuitive Intelligence
2. Inner Transmission
3. Guided Transferred Clairvoyancy
4. Telepathic Communication

Without a certain degree of development of intuitive intelligence, accurate inner transmission is difficult.

What is intuitive intelligence? How does it differ from mental intelligence? Mental intelligence is knowing through study, through experimentation. This uses the throat and the ajna chakras. Intuitive intelligence is knowing though direct inner perceptions or direct knowing. It doesn't require study. The disciple just simply knows. There are usually no inner images or visions. Intuitive intelligence utilizes the crown chakra. Intuitive intelligence is called *buddhi chitta* in the Buddhist tradition. Sometimes, it is called *awakening to the Truth.* Intuitive intelligence is one of the inner tools used frequently by MCKS.

Using mental intelligence alone is very slow. The mental plowing process is tedious. The materials are voluminous, not too clear, and are not straight to the point. Using the intuitive intelligence is much faster. It goes straight to the essence or the point. The components of the subject matter and the relationship of the components are clearly perceived. The subject materials are usually concise, clear and straight to the point.

Using intuitive intelligence alone is not enough. The concept or ideas that have been internally gathered by intuitive intelligence must still be analyzed, scrutinized and validated by using mental intelligence and actual experimentation.

In the writing of the book on Pranic Healing, MCKS partially saw already the structure and the contents with His intuitive intelligence. Validating these inner perceptions and putting them into words, would require more than five years.

## Inner Transmission

There *are* three major inner sources of information:

1. The inner transmission of the Teachings to MCKS by Lord Mahaguruji Mei Ling and his disciples;

2. The Teachings that were buried in the consciousness of MCKS from His ancient incarnations; and,

3. The concepts or ideas gathered by MCKS through the use of the faculty of intuitive intelligence.

The inner transmission of the Teachings from Lord Mahaguruji Mei Ling and his senior disciples is very subtle. Very often MCKS mistakenly thought that these ideas were developed by His own effort, through His own intuitive and mental faculties.

The inner transmission of the Teachings is done in the form of pure knowing. It does not have sound. It does not have color and does not have form. MCKS would receive the Teachings without any visual form and without any inner audible words. It was just pure knowing.

On a few occasions, the inner transmission came with inner visions. This mode of inner transmission utilizes the lower chakras below the crown chakra. In this mode of transmission, the disciple may see but may not understand what he or she is seeing. Being able to see does not necessarily mean being able to understand. It usually requires effort and time just to understand what has been seen internally.

Sensing where the sources of information came from is rather difficult, since the process involved is rather subtle. Also, the information may not come only from one source, but from a combination of the three sources.

Being able to distinguish information from inner transmission, from teachings learned from ancient lives, and from information gathered through intuitive and mental efforts is rather difficult. They are just so closely intertwined.

## Guided Transferred Clairvoyancy

Before their work with MCKS, both Mang Nenet and Mang Mike were already clairvoyant to a certain degree. Both could see the aura and chakras to a certain degree. Their understanding of the chakral system at that time was based on the seven chakras. They were not aware of the 11 chakras interpenetrating the body nor of the existence of the 12th chakra above the head. *Through guided transferred clairvoyance by Chohan Jig Mei Lingpa, Mang Dabon and the other senior disciples, they were able to see much more. Their clairvoyant skill improved many times through continuously working with MCKS in His experimentations on Pranic Healing and Arhatic Yoga.*

## Telepathic Communication

*In instances when clarification was required, the mode of communication shifted to telepathic communication. The physical instruments that were utilized were Mang Nenet and Mang Mike.*

MCKS would ask His thesis advisor Lord Mahaguruji Mei Ling or his senior disciples specific questions and specific answers were given by them through Mang Nenet and Mang Mike. *The physical instruments in many cases could not remember the content of the specific questions or the specific answers.*

Although Mang Nenet and Mang Mike were able to receive telepathic communications from the Teachers, they were not able to read the thoughts from ordinary people. In this case, the telepathic communication depends more predominantly on the skill of the spiritual teacher transmitting the messages and less on the skill of the disciple receiving the messages.

Chapter 10

# The Development of Modern Pranic Healing

## Pranic Healing Experiments

As stated earlier in the book, MCKS was already on the spiritual path as a teenager and had already studied and experimented on healing. His tendency to experiment continues even up to now.

From about 1982, for several years, MCKS visited Mang Mike and Mang Nenet regularly. It was necessary to give the body of Mang Mike many Pranic Healing treatments in order to make his body healthier and stronger.

The role of Mang Nenet and Mang Mike was to clairvoyantly monitor the experiments done by MCKS. As stated earlier, their clairvoyant vision was based on guided transferred clairvoyancy by Mang Dabon or Chohan Jig Mei Lingpa and in some instances, by other disciples of Lord Mahaguruji Mei Ling. For the sake of clarification, Mang Nenet practiced healing by prayer. Mang Mike was a psychic reader. He was not a healer.

As stated in Chapter Nine, in instances when clarification or additional information was required, MCKS would ask specific questions to His thesis advisor Lord Mahaguruji Mei Ling or his assistants - his senior disciples. Specific answers were given by them through Mang Nenet or Mang Mike.

The help through guided transferred clairvoyance, the clarifications and instructions were priceless. It must be stated that MCKS' Spiritual Thesis Advisor was the Lord Mahaguruji Mei Ling. In his Egyptian incarnation he was the Chief High Priest Nefertem, who was also *Born of the Lotus Flower*, and is considered to be the Egyptian *Deity of Healing and Aromatherapy.*

*MCKS visited Mang Mike regularly and would ask him to clairvoyantly monitor His healing experiments. In order to validate the findings, MCKS traveled every month to Cebu City to clairvoyantly cross-check the experiments with Mang Nenet. These two clairvoyants were not aware that their findings were being cross-checked against each other. Healing experiments were also done on many patients.*

After clairvoyantly observing what was happening with the experiments, Mang Mike would ask MCKS what He was doing. MCKS had to explain to him the healing technique that was being used. In some instances, the healing technique to be used was explained to Mang Mike before the experiment. Then, he would be asked to clairvoyantly monitor. These included the experiments on color pranas. At that time, Mang Mike and Mang Nenet did not know anything about the properties of color pranas.

*It has to be emphasized again, that the role of Mang Nenet and Mang Mike was just to clairvoyantly monitor the experiments being done by MCKS. The conceptualization, formulation, development and synthesis of the Pranic Healing Concepts and Principles, Techniques and Methodologies were done by MCKS through the utilization of both intellectual faculty and intuitive intelligence.*

## Union of Science and Spirituality

At the present moment, science sometimes seems to be incompatible with spirituality. What we call science is actually physical science. What we call spirituality is actually inner sciences or sciences not dealing with the physical world. The process of the union between science and spirituality is already in progress. This can be seen in the field of quantum physics merging with mysticism, in homeopathy, in acupuncture, feng shui, chi kung, vibrational medicine and others.

*Pranic Healing and Arhatic Yoga are examples of the union between science and spirituality. This trend is inevitable and will become stronger in the future.*

There is a clear distinction between spirituality and religion. Religion tends to be sectarian. It tends to be based on belief, and tends to be partially distorted by some of the followers of the founder. In some instances, religion tends to be the cause of much suffering due to war, while spirituality deals with the inner sciences. *Although there should be a separation between religion and state, there should be no separation between state and spirituality.*

## Different Healing Arts and Modern Pranic Healing

The reader must remember that in thesis writing, the thesis advisor only advises or helps. The thesis writer must do the bulk of the work. Easy or short cut approaches were not permitted. *MCKS had to sweat it out.*

The development of Modern Pranic Healing was extremely difficult. Healing was an art not a science. Transforming the healing arts into a science required enormous effort. Another factor to be considered is that in ancient times, the disciples had to do their spiritual or yogic practice for many years before they were able to heal. The task of MCKS was to study the different healing arts, experiment with them, validate them and find out the mechanism or the "how and why" of these healing arts. *MCKS' job was also to develop a very effective healing system which ordinary people can learn in just a short period of time. This was quite a herculean task.*

For the reader to understand what MCKS is driving at, various theories about the principles of healing from different schools of healing arts are mentioned. Some say that healing is based on faith only, some say it is placebo, some say it is based on internal chi and some say it is based on animal magnetism and etc. There are many healing arts from different parts of the world:

1. shamanic healing
2. Amazonian healing
3. Chinese medical chi kung
4. Rosicrucian healing
5. Reiki
6. magnetic healing
7. others

## Shamanic Healing

Shamanic healing uses branches of trees or the feather of an eagle for sweeping. Sometimes they use their mouth for sucking. With their inner vision they may see "insects" or "bugs". What exactly they are sucking out or are sweeping away is not clearly known to them. If you ask them, they would probably say they are sweeping away or sucking out "bad spirits". For students with Pranic Healing background, of course, it is obvious that they are sweeping or sucking out diseased energy.

The sucking technique is also very dangerous. A shaman once used the sucking technique to heal a German woman of breast cancer. The woman was healed, but the shaman died. The shamans also blow on the affected part. What exactly are they blowing out? For Pranic Healers it is quite clear that they are actually energizing by transferring pranic energy or the breath of life to the affected part.

## Amazonian Healing of Brazil

A woman who was doing missionary work in the Amazon in Brazil related an interesting story. If somebody was sick, the shaman would ask for the strongest young men to volunteer. The shaman would perform "sweeping" on the whole body of the patient and throw something to the strong young men. After that the young men were instructed to dip into the river. For a person with Pranic Healing background, it is rather amazing that general sweeping is also practiced in the Amazon. And that the young men were used as a substitute for a bowl of water and salt.

## Rosicrucian Healing

Rosicrucian healing is called Rosicrucian Contact Treatment. It is based on deep breathing. Vital life force is directed to the ganglia of the spine. *This vital life force is not directed to the chakras.* Rosicrucian healing is very simple and also effective. Rosicrucian Contact Treatment is taught by AMORC - The Ancient Mystical Order of Rosae Crucis. Due to a confidentiality agreement, MCKS cannot elaborate more on Rosicrucian healing. MCKS used His Christian name, not His Chinese name, when studying with AMORC.

## Reiki

According to a Reiki Master who studied with Phyllis Furamoto, Reiki uses attunement during initiation and symbols during healing. Practitioners of Reiki use symbols to connect to the Reiki energy.

*MCKS has not studied Reiki.* Therefore, the preceding paragraph is based on the statement of a Reiki Master.

According to that Reiki practitioner, Reiki does not contain:

a. Sensitizing
b. Scanning
c. Increasing Receptivity
d. General Sweeping (General Cleansing)
e. Localized Sweeping (Localized Cleansing)
f. Energizing using "hand chakra" technique or with Pranic Breathing
g. Stabilizing
h. Cutting and Releasing
i. Healing using Color Pranas
j. Energizing the Chakras

Practitioners also do not use a bowl of water and salt. Reiki does not recognize the factor of contamination from diseased energy.

## Yogic Healing

The following story is told in order for the readers to fully appreciate the teachings of the Pranic Healing system, so that they will understand what MCKS is driving at. One of the students of MCKS met a disciple of a well known swami. The disciple was impressed with MCKS' Pranic Healing. He explained that it was only after many years of studying and practicing yoga with the swami that they were taught how to do very simple healing like charging a glass of boiled water with pranic energy by using pranayama or yogic rhythmic breathing technique. The swamis do not teach their students the seven basic techniques in Pranic Healing, except for energizing. And their students were also not taught about the eleven chakras or about the use of color pranas or other principles and advanced techniques in Pranic Healing.

## Magnetic Healing

Magnetic healing was developed by a German doctor by the name of Franz Mesmer, a physician who was born on 23 May 1734. He studied medicine at the University of Vienna. Magnetic healing is based on "animal magnetism" which is an "invisible fluid" in the body. In the 1770's, he was *unjustly accused of fraud* by the physicians of Vienna and went to Paris, France. There, again, he encountered serious problems with the French medical establishment.* Later, Mesmerism became what is now known as hypnosis and the healing part became known as magnetic healing.

Just by reading the earlier paragraph you will notice that the idea of magnetic healing is rather difficult to comprehend. Nevertheless, magnetic healing as a healing art, produced some results, therefore, it required further investigation.

* Encyclopedia Britanica. The word "unjustly" was added by MCKS.

## Theosophy and Magnetic Healing

A few of the early theosophists practiced healing, to be exact, magnetic healing. Magnetic healing uses "animal magnetism" for healing. The use of this incorrect terminology has made the study and understanding of magnetic healing very confusing. This is why, when the theosophists transferred energy to a glass of water or an object, they used the term to "magnetize" the water or to "magnetize" the object. Theosophy contains vast, priceless ancient teachings but still, the healing art needed more clarity and development.

Magnetic healing also uses the term "passes" or "sweeping" on the entire body. Whether the practitioner understands the purpose is doubtful. The practitioner would *draw out* so called "blockages" with the left hand, absorb it into the body of the healer and release it through the right hand. This technique is very dangerous to the healer because of contamination from diseased energy. The book entitled, *The Etheric Double* by A.E. Powell states, "...the operator" (which is the term used for magnetic healer) "will *to withdraw (draw out)* from the patient congested or diseased etheric matter". The concept of diseased energy was rather nebulous in magnetic healing. It was not understood by most magnetic healers otherwise they would not have used the "drawing out technique".

Also, magnetic healers did not understand the purpose of making passes or sweeping the entire body. If they had understood the purpose of sweeping which was the cleansing or removing of diseased energy, they would have applied localized sweeping on the affected part instead of using the drawing out technique which is dangerous.

The practitioner of magnetic healing when sweeping the entire body, should adopt the "cupped hand position". Why? Based on clairvoyant observation, grayish light or diseased energy is scooped out of the body of the patient. This is good, but it is not enough. The health rays are still drooping or entangled. Therefore, the "spread finger position" had to be developed by MCKS and added when applying "general sweeping" in order to disentangle and strengthen the health rays so as to further accelerate the healing process of the body. The term "short circuiting" was also adopted from magnetic healing.

In *Esoteric Healing* by Alice Bailey, the terms magnetic healing and radiatory healing were used. These terms were formulated by Alice Bailey, not by her Spiritual Teacher. It was stated by Alice Bailey herself that the choice of words in writing the books was left to her discretion. In this case, because of the use of these terms, the development of the healing art into a science was much more difficult.

The book, *Esoteric Healing,* written through Alice Bailey by the Holy Master D.K., contains many priceless teachings and hints.

## Development of Modern Pranic Healing

Modern Pranic Healing had to be formulated and developed from the very bottom. Even though there were different healing arts from different esoteric and healing schools, many of the important concepts, principles, Seven Basic Techniques in Pranic Healing and terminologies in healing did not exist at that time. *During that time, healing was an art, not a science. MCKS' Spiritual Thesis was to develop the healing art into a fully developed healing science. There were no methodologies for healing different ailments of the different systems of the body.*

The Basic Concepts, Laws and Principles of Pranic Healing had to be clarified and explicitly formulated. The system of eleven chakras had to be developed. The properties of color pranas had to be developed and formulated. The specific methodologies or protocols for healing various physical ailments of the different systems of the body had to be developed. Later, the methodologies for healing psychological ailments had to be formulated.

## The Principle of Cleansing and Diseased Energy

In magnetic healing, they have "passes" or "sweeping". In shamanic healing in the Philippines, healers also do sweeping with branches of trees. In India, when grandchildren are sick, some grandmothers will sweep the child with a broom or with the branch of a tree. If the child asked the grandmother what she was doing, she will reply that she was "removing bad spirits". It is reported that in many cases, the children would get well. The question is why?

Based on experiments and clairvoyant observation, dirty grayish energy is removed from the subject when the sweeping is done. From this observation, the concept and the term *diseased energy* was created. When diseased energy was removed from the affected part, "light" from other parts of the body would move to the affected part and the patient would be relieved or healed. Based on the experiments and clairvoyant observation, *it was concluded by MCKS that the act of "general cleansing" and "localized cleansing" removes not only the diseased energy, but also facilitates the flow of pranic energy from other parts of the body to the affected part, thereby accelerating the natural healing process of the body.* The term sweeping was adopted into Pranic Healing. The terms and concepts of *general cleansing* and *localized cleansing* were formulated. The terms *general* and *localized* were added to the word sweeping. *General cleansing* is done through *general sweeping,* and *localized cleansing* is done through *localized sweeping.*

The concept of diseased energy and the concepts of general cleansing and localized cleansing seem obvious to the readers. You have to understand, before Isaac Newton, billions of people had seen apples or objects fall to the ground. But it was Isaac Newton who formulated the Law of Gravity. In ancient India, hundreds of millions or billions of grandmothers healed their grandchildren with branches or brooms, but they did not understand the principle behind what they were doing. *It was necessary for MCKS to explain and put emphasis on the very important concept of diseased energy.*

## The Principle of Contamination from Diseased Energy

In magnetic healing, the magnetic healer would draw out diseased energy through the left hand, absorb it into the body and release it through the right hand. A healer who understands the Principle of Diseased Energy and Principle of Contamination would never practice this technique since it is dangerous to the health of the healer. *The Principle of Contamination from diseased energy had to be explicitly formulated and emphasized in order for future Pranic Healers to avoid the danger of contamination.*

*The Principle of Decontamination also had to be emphasized for reasons of "energy hygiene".* This is done by washing the hands with water and salt *during and after* healing in order to minimize and remove contamination from diseased energy. In some instances, if the healer has engaged in previous activities that may have dirtied his hands, *it is also advisable for the healers to wash their hands before healing a patient, in order to avoid contaminating the patient.* Sometimes, the washing of the hands has to be done up to the elbow area. If the Pranic Healer has healed many patients in one setting, then the Pranic Healer should take a shower with water and salt or bath with water and salt.

## Diseased Energy Disposal Unit

It is necessary to dispose of the diseased energy properly instead of just throwing it anywhere in the healing room. A bowl of water and salt as a disposal unit must be used. Water is used to absorb the diseased energy and salt to disintegrate it. Earlier, MCKS used the term, *bioplasmic waste disposal unit.* This term is too long and difficult to understand and can be shortened to just *disposal unit.*

## The Principle of Energizing

Some Chinese martial artists including chi kung practitioners practice an exercise called "Reaching for the

Sky". One hand is raised upward and the other hand faces downward with the palm flat. They would alternate this position. The question is why?

Earlene Chaney, the wife of Dr. Robert Chaney of Astara did miraculous healing by raising her left arm upward, with her palm facing upward. Then, she would raise her right hand and direct it toward the patient. Many patients were miraculously healed. The question is, how and why? Magnetic healers also use the same pose. What was actually taking place?

Based on experiments and clairvoyant observation, *MCKS came to the conclusion that the hand has a hand chakra, the fingers have finger chakras. And the hand chakra and the finger chakras can absorb and project pranic energy.*

MCKS concluded that when the left hand is raised upward with the palm flat, the left hand chakra is absorbing air prana. When the right hand is directed to the affected part, the right hand chakra or right finger chakras are projecting pranic energy to the affected part.

Based on experiments and clairvoyant observation there was transference of "light" from the healer to the body of the patient.

MCKS had to clearly and explicitly state the concept that healing involves the transference of pranic energy from the healer to the body of the patient. This is why when the woman touched the hem of the robe of the Lord Jesus, "... the Lord Jesus said, 'Who touched me? Power has gone out of me.' The woman said, 'It is I, and I am healed'...".

(Luke 8:46-48) *It was not just faith alone. Healing involves the transference of healing energy from healer to patient. The Principle of Energizing was explicitly formulated.*

This act of transferring pranic energy is called "energizing". The concept of energizing through the hand-chakras technique is composed of two processes. *Drawing in or absorbing pranic energy from a chakra (not necessarily through the hand chakra) and projecting pranic energy through another chakra were explicitly formulated and stated.*

In Indian temples, deities can be seen in a pose with their left elbow bent up parallel to the ground, and the left palm facing upward. The right arm is raised partially upward with the right palm facing outward. Very often, there are paintings of flowers on the left palm and on the right palm. If you ask an Indian, "What is the meaning of the flower?" They will respond, "I do not know". But, if you ask an Indian, "What are the deities doing?" They will respond, "They are blessing".

The Sanskrit word chakra literally means wheel. In Bulgarian the word for wheel is also chakra. For the Indians to understand chakra as a flower is almost impossible. *MCKS had to explain to His Indian students that the flower actually symbolizes the hand chakra. Since the chakras rotate clockwise and counterclockwise alternately, the movement of these clockwise and counterclockwise energies produces an optical image of a lotus flower. The left hand chakra is used to absorb pranic energy and the right hand chakra is used to project pranic energy.* The Lord Buddha is also seen in a similar position.

*The statues of these deities have been part of the Indian culture and religion for thousands of years. Billions of Indians have seen these statues of the deities, but it was MCKS who gently explained to them that the flowers are actually hand chakras. The left hand is used to absorb pranic energy and the right hand to project pranic energy. The act of absorbing and projecting pranic energy is what they call blessing.*

## The Two Basic Principles in Pranic Healing

Based on many experiments and clairvoyant observation the Two Basic Principles of Pranic Healing were formulated:

1. Cleansing - removing the diseased energy;
2. Energizing - transferring of pranic energy to the patient.

## The Two Basic Laws in Pranic Healing

Based on the findings of many experiments, the Two Basic Laws of Pranic Healing were formulated:

1. The Law of Self Recovery

   In general the body is capable of healing itself at a certain rate.

2. The Law of Life Energy

   For life to exist, the body must have prana, chi or life energy. The natural healing process of the body can be accelerated by increasing life energy on the affected part(s) and on the entire body.

## The Principle of Stabilizing

On several occasions, it was noted that a short time after a patient was healed and relieved, the symptoms returned. This was very puzzling. Why would the symptoms return in less than an hour or in just a few hours? It was discovered that the projected pranic energy was "leaking out". In order to prevent the pranic energy from leaking out, the projected pranic energy had to be stabilized by projecting light sky blue pranic energy. The problem of the projected pranic energy leaking out was solved by this simple technique. The technique and terminology of "Stabilizing" were formulated.

Since projected pranic energy can be washed off by water, the patients are instructed not to take a bath or shower for one or two days. Rubbing the body with a slightly damp towel is permitted to clean the body.

## Faith and the Principle of Receptivity

It has been observed that even in healing simple cases, a few patients do not get well. The question is, why? It was clairvoyantly observed that when a patient does not believe in healing or does not like the healer the projected "light" or pranic energy *bounces back.* This can be felt by the Pranic Healer as a *pushing back sensation* against his hand. *From this, the Principle of Receptivity also known as the Principle of Internal Conductivity was clearly and explicitly formulated by MCKS. For healing to take place, the patient must be receptive or willing to absorb the projected pranic energy.*

Another term for receptivity is *faith*. When the woman touched the hem of the robe of the Lord Jesus, she was in a super receptive state. Because of that, there was a transfer of healing energy of the Lord Jesus to the woman. That was why the Lord Jesus said, "Power has gone out of me. Who touched me?" (Luke 8:45-48)

From this it can be clearly seen that healing occurred due to:

1. The *faith* or the receptivity of the woman; and,
2. The *transfer* of healing energy from the Lord Jesus to the woman.

## Faith and the Principle of Internal Conductivity

For electrical energy to pass through a physical object, that physical object must be electrically conductive. Electrical energy can pass through copper wire or gold wire, but not through a wire made of rubber or plastic. This is why another term for the Principle of Receptivity is the Principle of Internal Conductivity.

The Principle of Internal Conductivity states that the conductivity of the body and the subtle bodies depends on the psychological attitude of the person receiving the projected energy. *Super internal conductivity is called faith.*

There is a story in the Bible about a Roman soldier who approached the Lord Jesus and asked Him to please heal his servant who was sick. "The Lord Jesus, being kind and compassionate said, 'Let us go to your house'. The

Roman Soldier responded, 'No, Lord this is not necessary. If you just say he is healed, he will be healed'. The Lord Jesus said, 'I have not come across someone who has faith as strong as yours'. When the Roman soldier returned to his house his servant was healed". (Luke 7:1-10) Since the Roman soldier was super conductive to the healing energy from the Lord Jesus, the healing energy passed through his body into the body of the servant, resulting in the healing of the servant. *With the Principle of Internal Conductivity, we can scientifically understand this amazing story.*

## The Principle of Releasing

It has been experimentally observed that Pranic Healers have a problem healing their own relatives. This is due to the tendency of the Pranic Healer to be overly concerned or too anxious about the healing result. It has been clairvoyantly seen that there is an *energy cord* connecting the healer and patient. To prevent the projected pranic energy from returning to the healer it is necessary to visualize the energy cord being cut with an imaginary pair of scissors or an imaginary knife.

Although the idea of energy cord was a commonly known concept among esoteric students, it was not linked to the Principle of Releasing. *This important aspect of healing, the Principle of Releasing through cutting the energy cords, was formulated by MCKS.* Releasing is further accomplished by practicing detachment. Detachment is different from being indifferent.

## The Principle of Sensitizing

It has been noted by MCKS that when He directs His attention to His palm and fingers for a short period of time, He begins to feel something in His hand. When *attention* is directed to the palm and the fingers, the hand chakras become more active and brighter. In short, they became *activated.* This technique of "Sensitizing the Hands" was developed. It has been noticed that specifically directing of the attention to the palm and fingers works for most students, but not for all.

## Physical Exercises to Facilitate the Sensitizing of the Hands

To facilitate the sensitizing of the hands of the students, MCKS developed a set of six exercises that will clean and open up the energy channels of the spine, the shoulders, the arms, the hands, and the fingers:

1. spine exercise
2. hip exercise
3. neck exercise
4. shoulder exercise
5. elbow and fist exercise
6. wrist exercise

## The Principle of Scanning

Once the hands have been sensitized, they can be used as a device for feeling or *scanning* the outer aura, the inner aura, the health aura, the chakras and the energetic condition of the organs. Proficient advanced Pranic Healers can also use scanning to determine the condition of the organs inside the body. This requires a lot of practice and experience. The technique of sensing the energetic condition of the patient was termed scanning. It was further developed by MCKS.

## Increasing One's Pranic Energy Level by Connecting One's Tongue to the Palate

Connecting one's tongue to the palate is a yogic technique practiced by Chinese and Indian yogis. Often, the purpose is not clear. Based on experimentation and clairvoyant observation, *when the tongue is connected to the palate, the light around the body becomes bigger and brighter. In other words, the pranic energy level of the person increases.* The question is why? The answer is simple and obvious. The body has two main energy wirings or energy channels. One is at the back, inside the spine, and is called the *back energy channel.* The other one is in front and inside the body and is called the *front energy channel.* Since the body has to eat, the energy wiring circuit is broken. To make the circuit more complete, it is necessary to connect the tongue to the palate. A healer can easily increase his energy level just by connecting his tongue to the palate. The patient can also easily increase their energy level just by connecting their tongue to the palate. People who are stressed out and overworked may gradually increase their energy level by connecting their tongue to the palate and by doing deep rhythmic breathing or Pranic Breathing.

## Babies as Natural Born Yogis

When the baby is inside the womb of the mother, the tongue is connected to the palate. This can be seen in the ultrasound. Sometimes, the baby sucks its thumb. This is also seen in the ultrasound. The purpose is to complete the energy circuit so that its pranic energy level will be increased. This high pranic energy level is necessary for the complete and healthy development of the body of the baby which is growing at an extremely fast rate. After the baby has been born, the baby's tongue is usually connected to the palate. The baby habitually continues to suck its thumb. *It is better for the baby to suck its thumb than to use a rubber or plastic pacifier which is non-conductive.*

## The Principle of Pranic Breathing

Deep rhythmic breathing is called Pranayama in yoga. Pranayama or Pranic Breathing is divided into four parts:

1. Inhaling;
2. Retaining the breath after inhaling, which is called *full retention*;
3. Exhaling; and
4. Holding the breath after exhaling, this is called *empty retention.*

Pranic Breathing is part of the Kahuna tradition. They use Pranic Breathing 7-1-7-1 inhaling for 7 counts, holding the breath for 1 count and exhaling for 7 counts, holding the breath for 1 count.

The 7-1-7-1 Pranic Breathing Technique was also used by the practical Kabbalists. This simple Pranic Breathing technique was a closely guarded secret of the Kahunas and the practical Kabbalists.

Occultists of the Golden Dawn also use Pranic Breathing to generate energy. They use 6-3-6-3 breathing technique or 8-4-8-4 breathing technique. The ratio is 2:1. In India, a few yogic systems use the 6-3-6-3 Pranic Breathing technique. Most Indian yogic systems use other Pranic Breathing techniques.

## The Secret is in Empty Retention

The question is, why does deep rhythmic breathing or Pranayama generate tremendous amounts of pranic energy? Based on experiment and clairvoyant observation, it was noted that *tremendous amounts of pranic energy is drawn into the body during inhalation, only when it proceeded by empty retention or holding the breath after exhalation. This rediscovery is fantastic and is of great importance.*

## Simple Pranic Breathing: The Solution to Stress and Tiredness

Stress and fatique are pervasive problems in modern life. This modern epidemic can be solved if most people will just simply hold their breath for a few seconds after exhaling. *The body will be filled with tremendous amounts of pranic energy. People can work the whole day and still be feeling very strong and vibrant.* This simple rediscovery is the solution for the problem facing most people today. Most people are stressed out, tired and depleted. *The practice of connecting the tongue to the palate and the practice of holding the breath before inhalation will recharge the body. These simple techniques will energize and rapidly recharge their body. Empty retention must become part of their breathing pattern.*

## Chakras are Gates

Chakras are gates through which pranic energy can move in and out. The hands have hand chakras and finger chakras. The feet have sole chakras and toe chakras. These hands and feet chakras are important "gates" through which pranic energy can go in and out.

## Absorbing Air, Tree and Earth Pranas

The concept of chakras as gates, when combined with Pranic Breathing, developed the Pranic Technologies on how to absorb air, tree and earth pranas which are very simple. The linking of the concept of chakras as gates and Pranic Breathing was obvious or simply common sense.

The Pranic Technology for absorbing air prana into the body is:

1. Do this in a clean place.
2. Connect the tongue to the palate.
3. Raise your hands.
4. Be aware of the center of your palms and the rest of your body simultaneously.
5. Simultaneously do Pranic Breathing.
6. Do this for 10 to 20 breathing cycles.

The Pranic Technology for absorbing tree prana into the body is:

1. Do this in a clean place.
2. Connect the tongue to the palate.
3. Raise your hands and place them near the tree trunk.
4. Be aware of the center of your palms and the rest of your body simultaneously.
5. Simultaneously do Pranic Breathing.
6. Do this for 10 to 20 breathing cycles.

It is important to scan the tree to determine if it is healthy or not. Pranic Healers who are sensitive can easily determine this. Please change trees on a regular basis and please do not deplete the tree.

The Pranic Technology for absorbing ground prana into the body is:

1. Do this in a clean place.
2. Connect the tongue to the palate.
3. Remove your shoes and socks.
4. Be aware of the soles of your feet and the rest of your body.
5. Simultaneously do Pranic Breathing.
6. Do this for 10 to 20 breathing cycles.

It is important to emphasize that this be done in a clean place and on clean ground. Using this technique in a dirty place or on dirty ground will make the body of the practitioner very sick. Dirty energy will penetrate deep into the system of the practitioner. Some beaches in the world are extremely dirty. One must be cautious in practicing this technique. Do not practice in the following places:

1. stressful places
2. bars
3. on top of or near septic tanks
4. on former graveyard sites
5. on former battlefield areas
6. other dirty places

When doing these techniques, please move from location to location or else the surrounding plants may die.

*Please do not misuse Pranic Healing technology to vampirize the pranic energy of another person. The karmic penalties for such an offense are very heavy:*

1. *severe sickness*
2. *paralysis*
3. *extreme poverty*
4. *insanity*
5. *death*
6. *and others*

## Seven Basic Techniques in Pranic Healing

MCKS finally developed the Seven Basic Techniques in Pranic Healing:

1. Sensitizing the Hands

   Intermediate level:
   Sensitizing through Pranic Breathing

2. Scanning the inner aura of the body and its internal organs

3. Sweeping
   a. General sweeping - general cleansing
   b. Localized sweeping - localized cleansing

   Intermediate Level:
   Sweeping with Pranic Breathing

4. Increasing the receptivity of the patient

5. Energizing with prana

   Hand chakras technique
   a. Drawing in prana
   b. Projecting prana

   Intermediate Level:
   a. Energizing with Pranic Breathing
   b. Energizing with distributive sweeping

6. Stabilizing the projected pranic energy

7. Releasing the projected pranic energy

All the techniques have been tried and tested, and they work.

## Development of the Eleven Major Chakras System

What is generally accepted is the Seven Major Chakras System. Introducing the Eleven Major Chakras System was met with strong resistance from practitioners of the healing arts and from esoteric students.

How was the Eleven Major Chakras System developed? It was rather simple. There are different Seven Major Chakras Systems. A person with a clear mind will realize that these different systems are actually dealing with different seven major chakras. For the sake of clarification, one of the Seven Major Chakras Systems is based on the endocrine Glands:

1. Crown Chakra - Pineal Gland
2. Ajna Chakra - Pituitary Gland
3. Throat Chakra - Thyroid Glands
4. Heart Chakra - Thymus Gland
5. Solar Plexus Chakra - Pancreas
6. Sex Chakra - Testicles and Ovaries
7. Basic Chakra - Adrenal Glands

The other two commonly known chakras are:

1. Spleen Chakra
2. Navel Chakra

The remaining two chakras were derived through inner transmission, making a total of eleven chakras:

1. Forehead Chakra
2. Meng Mein Chakra

The existence of the eleven major chakras was validated through scanning, clairvoyant observation and experiments.

More than ten years after the book, *The Ancient Science and Art of Pranic Healing,* was published, MCKS came across certain passages in Indian holy books. In the *Bhagavad Gita* 5:13, the Lord Krishna mentioned about " . . . a city with nine gates", thereby hinting the existence of the nine major chakras.

The *Katha Upanishad,* stanza 5, mentions that ". . .there is a city with eleven gates", thereby hinting the existence of the eleven major chakras.

The traditional interpretation of the nine gates and eleven gates is "holes in the body". Why would the Maharishis or wise men of India waste their time by counting the holes in the body?

In the Kabbalistic Inverted Tree of Life, there are ten sephiroth or energy centers and one hidden, a total of eleven major chakras. The sephiroth are interpreted as corresponding to different parts of the body by the rabbis and the Kabbalists. They did not know that the sephiroth correspond to the eleven major chakras because the eleven major chakras system was not revealed before, to the public. The correspondence of the eleven sephiroth to the chakras was revealed by MCKS in His two books:

a. *The Universal and Kabbalistic Chakra Meditation on the Lords Prayer*, and,
b. *The Spiritual Essence of Man, The Chakras and the Kabbalistic Tree of Life.*

## Eleven Major Chakras and Their Functions

The eleven major chakras also correspond to certain important acupuncture points.

1. The *Crown Chakra* - GV20 - is located at the crown of the head. It controls and energizes the brain and the pineal gland. In Chinese acupuncture, "GV" pertains to the *Governor Channel* or *Governor Vessel.*

2. The *Forehead Chakra* - GV24 - is located at the center of the forehead. It controls and energizes the nervous system and also the pineal gland.

3. The *Ajna Chakra* - M-HN3 (*Yin Tang*) - is located between the eyebrows. It controls and energizes the pituitary gland and the endocrine glands.

4. The *Throat Chakra* - CV23 - is located in the throat area. It controls and energizes the thyroid glands. The abbreviation "CV" pertains to the *Conception Channel* or *Conception Vessel.*

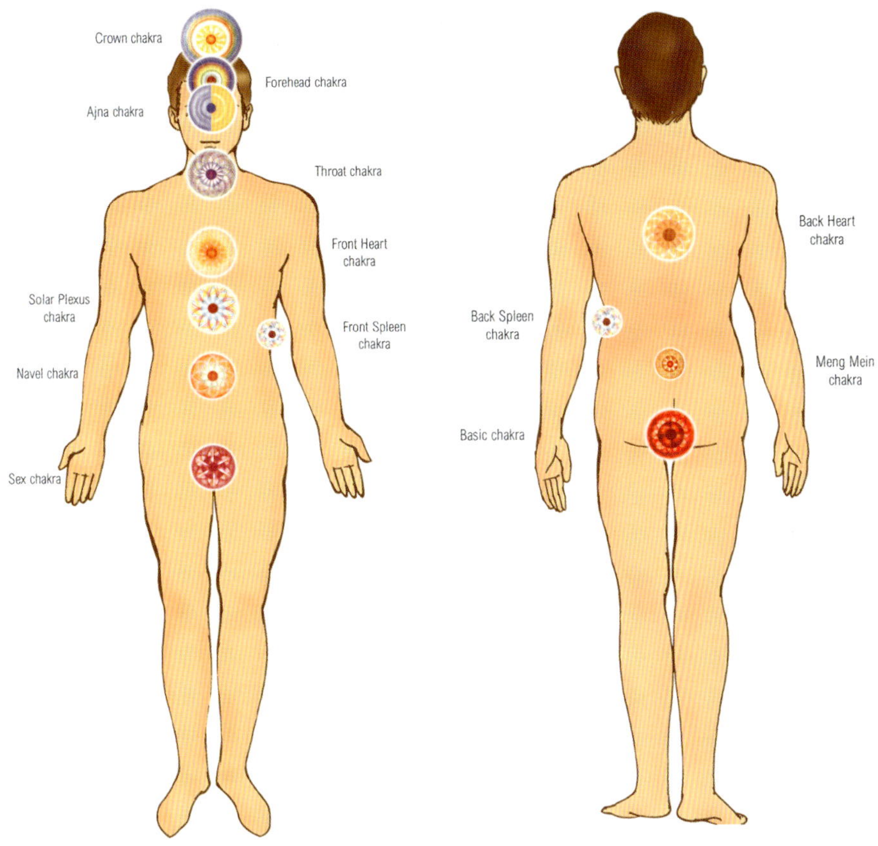


**The Eleven Major Chakras**

Major chakras are whirling energies that control and energize the major organs of the visible body.

* From The Spiritual Essence of Man by Master Choa Kok Sui.

5. The *Heart Chakra* - is composed of front and back heart. The *front heart chakra* - CV17 - is located in front of the heart. It controls and energizes the heart and thymus gland. The *back heart chakra* - GV11 - is located at the back of the heart. It controls and energizes the lungs, the heart and the thymus gland. This is why smoking is very bad for the heart.

6. The *Solar Plexus Chakra* - is composed of the front and back solar plexus. The *front solar plexus* - CV15 - is located at the hollow area between the ribs. It controls and energizes the diaphragm, pancreas, liver, stomach and to a certain degree, large and small intestines, appendix and other internal organs. The *back solar plexus* - GV 9 - is located at the back of the solar plexus, has the same functions as the front solar plexus. The solar plexus chakra also controls the heating and cooling system of the body.

7. The *Navel Chakra* - CV8 - is located on the navel. It controls and energizes the small and large intestines and appendix.

8. The *Spleen Chakra* is composed of front and back spleen. The *front spleen chakra* - SP16 - is located in front of the spleen. The *back spleen chakra* does not have a corresponding known acupuncture point. The spleen chakra controls and energizes the physical spleen. The spleen chakra absorbs and digests the air prana. The digested air prana or the color pranas are distributed to the other chakras. In other words, the spleen chakra energizes all the major chakras and the body.

9. The *Meng Mein Chakra* - GV4 - is located at the back of the navel. It controls and energizes the kidneys and the adrenal glands. It also controls the blood pressure.

10. The *Sex Chakra* - CV2 - is located on the pubic area. It controls and energizes the sex organs, including the urinary organs, except the kidneys.

11. The *Basic Chakra* - GV1 - is located at the base of the spine. It controls and energizes the skeletal and muscular system, blood, the adrenal glands, and the tissue of the body.

## Painting the Eleven Major Chakras

Initial clairvoyant investigation was done by Bishop Leadbeater in his book, *The Chakras.* His findings were revalidated by Mang Mike and Mang Nenet. The clairvoyant investigation of the eleven major chakras was directed by MCKS and was done by Mang Mike and Mang Nenet.

In order to study the eleven major chakras, the clairvoyant monitor had to "will" the chakra to "slow down". Guided transferred clairvoyance was done by Mang Dabon, or the senior disciple(s) of Lord Mahaguruji Mei Ling, to the two clairvoyant monitors, Mang Mike and Mang Nenet. Their findings were cross checked against each other without their knowledge. The initial color drawings of the eleven major chakras were done separately by Mang Mike and Mang Nenet. They were later done by a clairvoyant artist.

## Who Should Not Heal

The following people should not do healing to avoid contaminating the patient:

a. heavy smokers
b. alcoholics
c. drug addicts
d. others with dirty energy

## When A Healer Should Not Heal

To avoid contaminating the patient it is important for a healer to know when not to heal:

1. A healer should not heal when he is sick or suffering from general weakness. This is to avoid the transference of diseased energy to the patient.

2. A healer should not also heal when he is feeling very angry or irritated because the projected pranic energy will be contaminated with anger and other negative emotions. This may cause the patient's condition to become worse.

## Protocol for Basic Problems Encountered in Pranic Healing

The following are the basic problems encountered in Pranic Healing:

1. In areas where there is Pranic Depletion: cleansing and energizing are applied to the affected areas. The emphasis is on *energizing.*

2. In the areas where there is Pranic Congestion diseased and congested energy is removed or extracted from the affected areas. This is followed by projecting prana to the treated area. The emphasis is on *cleansing* or decongesting.

3. A malfunctioning chakra is restored by simply cleansing and energizing it with prana.

4. Drooping and entangled health rays are disentangled and strengthened by general sweeping with Pranic Breathing using the spread fingers position.

5. Blocked meridians or energy channels are cleansed and energized.

6. Prana which leaks out through holes in the outer aura is sealed.

7. Specific types of prana are applied to produce specific results. Certain illnesses need a specific type or types of prana to produce faster results. This is taught in Advanced Pranic Healing.

## Five Things to Avoid in Pranic Healing

To make Pranic Healing safer, the following guidelines must be followed:

1. Do not apply too intense and too much prana on infants, very young children, the very weak and elderly patients.

2. Do not energize the eyes directly.

3. Do not directly and intensely energize the heart for a long time. It is quite sensitive and delicate. The heart should be energized through the back heart chakra.

4. In general, do not energize the meng mein chakra of infants, small children, and older people.

5. In general, do not energize the spleen chakra of infants or children because they may faint as a result of Pranic Congestion.

## Avoid Energizing with the Eyes

Some healers use their eyes in energizing patients. Because the diseased energy is absorbed by the eyes, this is not advisable. Also, it is not advisable to energize directly from your major chakra to the diseased part of the patient for the same reason. It is better to energize with the hand chakra or finger chakra since the hands and fingers are easier to clean and are not very delicate compared to the eyes, brain or heart.

## General Procedure in Pranic Healing

Since it is not possible to give a methodology or protocol for all types of ailments, it is necessary to give a general procedure that can be followed by Pranic Healers for dealing with ailments that may not be found in MCKS' books.

1. Smile and establish rapport with the patient to enhance his receptivity. Observe and interview him.

2. Scan the affected parts, the vital organs, major chakras, and the spine.

3. Instruct him to assume the receptive pose.

4. Apply general sweeping.

5. Do localized sweeping on the affected areas.

6. Rescan the affected parts. In case of Pranic Congestion, scan to determine whether the congestion has been significantly reduced or not. For Pranic Depletion, scan to determine if the inner aura of the affected parts has become a little bigger or has partially normalized.

7. In simple cases, sweeping or cleansing is sometimes sufficient to heal the patient.

8. Before energizing, make the patient receptive in order to facilitate the absorption and assimilation of the projected pranic energy.

9. Energize the affected parts with prana.

10. Get feedback from your patient. If there is some pain left, ask for the exact spots and rescan those areas.

11. Do more sweeping and energizing.

12. If the part is highly over-energized, do distributive sweeping to prevent possible Pranic Congestion.

13. Rescan the treated area to determine whether the affected area has been sufficiently decongested or energized. Thoroughness is the key to dramatic healing or very fast healing.

14. In Pranic Congestion, cleansing is emphasized. In Pranic Depletion, energizing is emphasized.

15. Stabilize the projected prana. This is very important.

16. Release the projected pranic energy by visualizing the etheric cord or energy cord of light linking you and the patient being cut by an imaginary pair of scissors or knife.

17. Instruct your patient not to wash the part that has just been treated for about 12 hours; otherwise, the symptoms may recur. Water absorbs some of the pranic energy that has been projected to the affected part.

18. Patients suffering from severe ailments or general weakness should not take a shower or a bath for about 24 hours after Pranic Healing treatment.

This is to enable the body to gradually absorb and assimilate the pranic energy that has been projected.

## Critical Factors in Pranic Healing

1. The patient must be scanned and rescanned thoroughly and accurately.

2. The patient's energy body must be thoroughly cleansed to increase the rate of healing and to avoid radical reaction.

3. The patient must be energized sufficiently with prana. Insufficient energizing would produce only slight improvement or a slow rate of healing.

4. Stabilize the projected prana to prevent it from escaping or leaking out.

5. When the healer is calm and detached, the projected energy is released and the etheric cord linking the healer and patient is automatically cut. To be sure, cut the energy cord to release.

## Insulating Garments

Materials such as silk, rubber, and leather goods tend to act as partial insulators to prana. Patients should be requested to wear cotton clothes since they make the projection of prana on them easier.

## How Frequently Should Healing Be Done?

In order to achieve the proper result in healing, it is necessary to give Pranic Healing treatments to the patient at the right frequency. This depends on several factors:

1. The severity and the acuteness of the ailment;

2. The rate of pranic consumption;

3. The delicateness and importance of the part being treated; and,

4. The age and health condition of the patient.

## Holistic or Integrated Approach in Healing

Although Pranic Healing can produce many amazing results, it has its limitations. *Proper diet and physical exercise are also necessary.* At times, the intake of herbs or medicinal drugs, change in lifestyle, emotional therapy or surgery is required. It is important to maintain one's objectivity and to have proper perspective of what the other types of healing can do. Fanaticism and going to the extremes should be avoided.

*Pranic Healing is not intended to replace orthodox medicine, but rather to complement it. If an ailment is severe, or if symptoms persist, please consult immediately a medical doctor and a reputable Pranic Healer.*

## Pranic Distant Healing

There are two principles in Pranic Distant Healing.

1. The Principle of Interconnectedness

   The mechanism of the Pranic Distant Healing is similar to that of the telephone. The healer and the patient are interconnected because their etheric or energy bodies are parts of the Earth's etheric body.

*The planetary etheric body is whole, unbroken and continuous; of this etheric body, those of the healer and of the patient are integral, intrinsic parts....The channels of relationship can be conductors of many different types of energy, transmitted by the healers to the patient.*

- Esoteric Healing, *Alice Bailey*

2. The Principle of Directability

   Pranic energy follows where your intention is focused.

## Principle of Lag Time

The Principle of Lag Time means that the rate of healing of the energy body is much faster than that of the visible physical body. Therefore, in some cases, the patient may not experience immediate relief or cure because the visible physical body heals at a slower pace than the energy body. This delay or lag time in relief or cure is especially common in more severe cases. The degree of delay or lag time will depend on the degree of damage, the age, the physical condition and the receptivity of the patient.

## Self Pranic Healing

Self Pranic Healing is based on principles and techniques in Pranic Healing.

1. Recharging the Physical Body:

    a. Apply localized sweeping on the front solar plexus chakra about 30 times.

    b. Apply localized sweeping on the back solar plexus chakra about 30 times.

    c. Wash your hands thoroughly.

    d. Put your fingers on your solar plexus chakra.

    e. Do 6-3-6-3 pranic breathing about 7 to 12 times.

    f. Simultaneously be aware of the whole body.

    g. Apply distributive sweeping on the front solar plexus chakra to avoid congestion.

    h. Stabilize the projected pranic energy on the solar plexus chakra.

    This technique for recharging the physical body can be done by people who are overworked and stressed out. It may also be utilized by people who are sick to accelerate the healing process of their body. They can do this once a day or two to three times per day depending on their condition.

2. Recharging the Brain

When you are mentally exhausted and you still have a lot of work, you can do the following:

a. Wash your hands first.

b. Apply localized sweeping on the brain area about 30 times.

c. Apply localized sweeping on your back head for about 30 times

d. Wash your hands again.

e. Curl your fingers and place them at the back of your head. Then do deep Pranic Breathing for 5 to 10 times to energize the entire head. Simultaneously, be aware of the whole brain including the eyes. This is to facilitate the distribution of pranic energy to the different parts of the head.

f. If you feel a bit dizzy or over-energized, apply some sweeping on the head to remove the excess energy.

## Water And Salt Bath

It is advisable to take a bath with warm water and salt on a regular basis. This is extremely helpful to remove stress energy and dirty energy. About 10 drops of lavender oil may be added to the salt.

For people who are sick, this suggestion is very important to remove diseased and dirty energy. They may take a bath with warm water and salt once per day, or even several times a day.

## The Great Sacrifice

To finish His Spiritual Thesis, it required extreme one pointedness, which inevitably resulted in the breaking down of His marriage. The price paid to develop and spread Modern Pranic Healing was personally very high.

MCKS' former wife is a good person. In the process of trying to preserve the marriage and family, sometimes she was verbally hard on some people. This was not done out of malice, but simply to protect the unity of the family. Even up to now, she is very helpful to strangers and is generous to friends in need.

## The Birth of Modern Pranic Healing

*The preparatory work for developing Modern Pranic Healing started when MCKS was just a teenager. It took more than 18 years to develop Modern Pranic Healing.*

*For about five years (1983-1987), when the main bulk of Modern Pranic Healing was being validated, conceptualized, synthesized, formulated, systematized, and developed, MCKS "ate, drank and slept Pranic Healing". This was one of the toughest and most difficult part of His life.*

*To formulate and develop Modern Pranic Healing from a zygote state (fertilized egg) to adulthood in a few years time was just almost impossible. The completion of the Spiritual Thesis was extremely difficult. The effort required was monumental.*

*Modern Pranic Healing as a science was finally born in late 1987 when the book,* The Ancient Science and Art of Pranic Healing, *by Master Choa Kok Sui was finally published. At present, MCKS' book on Pranic Healing is published in over thirty languages.*

Advanced Pranic Healing or Pranic Healing using color pranas was also included in one of the chapters in the first edition of this book.

Based on hindsight, the title, *The Ancient Science and Art of Pranic Healing,* was incorrect. Healing in ancient times was an art and cannot be compared to Modern Pranic Healing at all. Therefore, the book was re-titled *Miracles Through Pranic Healing* because so many amazing results were produced through the use of Modern Pranic Healing.

As stated by St. Augustine, "Miracles do not happen in contradiction to nature, but only to that which is known to us about nature".*

* Master Choa Kok Sui, Miracles Through Pranic Healing, 3rd ed. (Philippines, Institute for Inner Studies, Inc., 1997).

Note: The materials in this chapter on "The Development of Modern Pranic Healing", up to this page have been substantially extracted from MCKS' book, The Ancient Science and Art of Pranic Healing, which has been re-titled as Miracles through Pranic Healing.

Chapter 11

# The Development of Advanced Pranic Healing



## Color Pranas and Their Properties

Air prana, when digested by the spleen chakra, produces red, orange, yellow, green, blue and violet prana. Ground prana is absorbed through the sole chakras. It goes up to the basic chakra. A portion of the ground prana is directed up to the spine and the other chakras while a larger portion is directed to the perineum minor chakra, to the navel chakra, then to the spleen chakra where it is broken down and the color pranas are distributed to the other chakras.

The research done by Leadbeater did not mention anything about indigo prana. Does indigo prana exist? The answer is yes. The question is how come Leadbeater did not notice the existence of indigo prana? The answer is that indigo prana lasts less than a split second before it breaks down into the other six color pranas - violet prana, blue prana, green prana, yellow prana, orange prana and red prana. Without guided transferred clairvoyance by the Teacher or his senior disciples, this would have never have been noticed. Indigo prana is not used for healing because indigo prana is destructive to the physical body of most people.

The properties of color prana are based on the teaching from Lord Mahaguruji Mei Ling, and through experiments and clairvoyant observations. *The properties and the applications of the color pranas in Pranic Healing were conceptualized and formulated by MCKS.*

## Nine Years of Hard Work

MCKS established a Pranic Healing Center in Kamuning Street. He was healing about 10 to 20 patients almost every afternoon from Monday through Saturday. Mang Mike was also healing other patients. This was done to further validate the Pranic Healing techniques for MCKS' *Advanced Pranic Healing* book. This continued for about two years.

Writing the *Advanced Pranic Healing* book was also very difficult, considering that healing methodologies or protocols had to be developed for different ailments for each system of the body. This was a gigantic task. MCKS had to regularly go and stay in a convent with the nuns who had studied Pranic Healing, in order to write and finish the book on Advanced Pranic Healing. The Catholic nuns were very supportive and gave Him the solitude needed to finish the book. MCKS is very appreciative of the kindness that He received from these Catholic nuns.

The research on Advanced Pranic Healing using color pranas started in about 1983. The initial findings were published in 1987, in one of the chapters of the book entitled, *The Ancient Science and Art of Pranic Healing. It took about nine years of hard work to develop Advanced Pranic Healing - Pranic Healing using Color Pranas. In 1992, the book on* Advanced Pranic Healing *was finally published. The healing art became a fully matured science, Advanced Pranic Healing.*

At present, *Advanced Pranic Healing* by MCKS has been published in over nineteen languages.

It must be clearly stated that Chinese medical chi kung, magnetic healing, Reiki, shamanic healing or other healing schools do not use Advanced Pranic Healing or color pranas in healing. Advanced Pranic Healing or Pranic Healing using color pranas was conceptualized, formulated and developed by Master Choa Kok Sui.

To give the reader an idea of why it took nine years to develop Advanced Pranic Healing, this chapter will contain a very brief summary of the book.

## Properties of Color Pranas and Applications

### Red Prana

Properties:

1. Strengthening
2. Warm
3. Expansive
4. Dilating
5. Distributive (improves circulation)
6. Constructive - rapid tissue or cellular repair
7. Sustain the visible physical body
8. Vitalizes the blood, tissue, and the skeletal system of the body
9. Stimulating and activating

Applications:

1. Strengthening sluggish and weakened organs or parts.
2. Dilating blood vessels and air tubes
3. Improving circulation
4. Allergy
5. Internal and external wounds
6. General tiredness or weakening
7. Paralysis
8. Reviving unconscious patients
9. Reviving or prolonging the life of dying patients

## Orange Prana

Properties:

1. Expelling
2. Eliminative
3. Decongesting
4. Cleansing
5. Loosening - loosens diseased energy
6. Melting
7. Extracting and abstracting
8. Splitting, exploding and destructive

Applications:

1. Expelling or elimination of waste, toxins, germs, and diseased energy.
2. Allergy
3. Kidney and bladder ailments
4. Constipation
5. Menstrual problems
6. Removing blood clot
7. Arthritis
8. Cyst
9. Cold, cough, and lung problems

## Green Prana

Properties:

1. Breaking down
2. Digestive
3. Decongesting
4. Cleansing
5. Detoxifying
6. Disinfecting
7. Dissolving
8. Loosening of diseased energy matter
9. Destruction or breaking down of dead and diseased cells

Applications:

1. Breaking down blood clot
2. Disinfecting
3. Cold
4. Fever
5. Used in localized sweeping for decongesting and loosing stubborn diseased energy

## Yellow Prana

Properties:

1. Cohesion or cementing
2. Assimilating, multiplying, and growing
3. Stimulating effect on the nerve (subtle yellow prana from the crown chakra)
4. Initiating or starting
5. Necessary for strong and healthy tissue, organs and bones

Applications:

1. Broken bones
2. Skin problems
3. Cellular repair
4. Developing strong healthy tissue, organs and bones
5. Improving assimilation

### Blue Prana

Properties
1. Disinfecting and disinflaming
2. Inhibiting
3. Localizing and contracting
4. Soothing and mild anesthetic
5. Cooling
6. Pliability or flexibility
7. Blood clotting

Applications:
1. Ailments due to infection
2. Removing of pain
3. Reducing inflammation
4. Inhibiting chakras, organs, and motor action
5. Inducing rest and sleep
6. Stopping bleeding
7. Bringing down fever

## Violet Prana

Violet prana has the properties of all the other five pranas combined and is potent. It is used for severe types of ailments.

Both white prana and violet prana have the properties of all the color pranas. The difference is that violet prana has a greater penetrating effect and is easier to assimilate than white prana. Therefore, violet prana has a faster effect than white prana.

## Electric Violet Pranic Energy

There are two types of violet pranic energy: ordinary violet pranic energy and electric violet pranic energy. The former appears as luminous violet which is derived from the surrounding prana such as air, ground, and solar pranas. The latter appears as brilliant white light with light violet at the periphery. This is derived from the higher soul where its entry point is the crown chakra, and hence is called divine energy or soul energy.

Electric violet pranic energy has the properties of all the other color pranas and is many times more powerful than ordinary violet pranic energy. It has a rapid regenerating effect in damaged organs and nerves, and also very strong disinfecting effect. Electric violet pranic energy has a consciousness of its own and is very effective for rapid healing of severe ailments.

## Golden Pranic Energy

When electric violet pranic energy comes in contact with the energy body, it gradually turns into golden prana. The golden prana, when absorbed by the physical body, becomes light red. Golden prana has properties almost similar to those of electric violet prana. Golden prana is milder and less fluidic than electric violet prana. Golden prana has less cleansing effect than electric violet prana. *In general, it is better to use electric violet prana for general energizing, and golden prana for localized energizing.*

## Advanced Pranic Healing Techniques

### Basic-Hand Chakras Technique

Basic-hand chakras technique can be used to project the following color pranas:

1. red prana
2. orange prana
3. yellow prana
4. orange-red prana (more of orange prana, less of red prana)
5. orange-yellow prana (less of orange prana, more of yellow prana)

Light whitish orange-red prana is used for the rapid healing of fresh wounds. Light whitish orange-yellow prana is used for rapid healing of broken bones and torn tendons.

### Throat-Hand Chakras Technique

The throat-hand chakras technique is used to project the following color pranas:

1. blue prana
2. green prana
3. greenish-blue prana

Light whitish green-blue prana is used to treat fresh burns, infections, inflammations, food poisoning, and also to stop bleeding.

## Crown-Hand Chakras Technique

The crown-hand chakras technique is used to project the following color pranas:

1. ordinary violet prana
2. ordinary bluish-violet prana (less of blue prana, more of violet prana)
3. ordinary greenish-violet prana (less of green prana, more of violet prana)
4. greenish-yellow prana
5. electric white prana (divine healing energy)
6. electric violet prana (divine healing energy)
7. golden prana (divine healing energy)

## Advanced General Sweeping

General sweeping can be done with light whitish green prana in order to loosen the diseased energy and to facilitate its removal.

## Advanced Localized Sweeping, Loosening or Decongesting

If the diseased energy is difficult to remove or is quite stubborn, it is advisable to apply localized sweeping alternately with light whitish green prana and light whitish orange prana to loosen the stubborn diseased energy. Please note the sequence: green prana first and then orange prana. This approach is much safer. If cleansing is done properly on the affected part, there will be rapid partial or complete relief. This technique is much faster than ordinary localized sweeping. In some instances, from the ordinary person's viewpoint, the effect is almost miraculous.

The sex chakra, basic chakra, and the minor chakras on the arms and legs can be cleansed rapidly and thoroughly by sweeping alternately with light whitish green prana and light whitish orange prana.

Do not use orange prana on delicate organs or on prohibited areas.

## Cleansing Delicate Organs

If the affected part is quite delicate or is near a delicate organ, apply localized sweeping with light whitish green. Or apply localized sweeping alternately with light whitish green prana and ordinary light whitish violet prana. These techniques also produce fast relief and are quite safe.

## Principles of Pranic Healing

For healing to be considered as a science the concepts or principles must be clearly stated and labeled:

1. Principle of Life Energy or Prana
2. Principle of Pervasiveness
3. Principle of Diseased Energy
4. Principle of Transmitability
5. Principle of Contamination
6. Principle of Controllability
7. Principle of Cleansing and Energizing
8. Principle of Radical Reaction
9. Principle of Receptivity
10. Principle of Stabilizing
11. Principle of Releasing
12. Principle of Correspondence
13. Principle of Interconnectedness
14. Principle of Directability

## Preventive Healing

There is a saying, "An ounce of prevention is worth a pound of cure". In Preventive Healing, there are nine factors to be considered:

1. proper diet
2. proper breathing
3. sufficient proper exercise
4. proper etheric hygiene
5. proper emotions and thoughts (emotional and mental hygiene)
6. proper human relationships
7. proper livelihood
8. proper lifestyle
9. preventive Pranic Healing treatment

Harboring or explosively expressing negative feelings for a prolonged period may manifest as:

1. glaucoma
2. migraine headache
3. acute sinusitis
4. hyperthyroidism
5. respiratory ailments
6. heart ailments
7. diabetes
8. gastric or intestinal ulcer
9. high cholesterol
10. infected liver (negative emotion weakens the body and the liver, thereby making it susceptible to infection.)
11. constipation
12. twisted intestine

13. damage kidneys
14. hypertension
15. rheumatoid arthritis
16. cancer and others

## Proper Lifestyle

The lifestyle of a person is an important health factor. Undesirable habits and excessiveness should be avoided, like:

1. smoking of cigarettes or tobacco
2. alcoholism
3. drug abuse
4. excessive work - hard work or industriousness is indeed a virtue but working fourteen to sixteen hours a day for several months or years is definitely excessive and definitely bad for the health and bad for family life.
5. excessive fun - to have fun is great but too much fun or too much night life for a prolonged period is quite exhausting and will definitely have adverse effect on the health.

## General Applications

The chapter on General Applications contains Advanced Pranic Healing Techniques and many Pranic Healing Treatments.

1. Activating the Chakra
2. Inhibiting the Chakra
3. Strengthening
4. Inhibiting
5. Localizing
6. Treating Infants and Old People
7. Relieving Pain: Blue Prana
8. Headache
9. Migraine Headache
10. Toothache
11. Pyorrhea
12. Energizing the Basic Chakra and the Perineum Chakra
13. How to Strengthen the Legs
14. How to Strengthen the Arms
15. Broken Bone: Orange-Yellow Pranas
16. Concussion
17. Contusion
18. Back Injury
19. Fresh Burns: Green and Blue Pranas
20. Old Minor Burns: Green and Red Pranas
21. Old Severe Burns: Green and Red Pranas
22. How to Stop Bleeding: Blue Prana
23. Old Wounds: Green and Red Pranas
24. Instantaneous Healing of Fresh Wounds: Orange and Red Pranas

25. Regeneration: Green-yellow Prana, Green-violet Prana or Light Whitish Green, Light Whitish Orange, and Light Whitish Red Orange-yellow Prana
26. Rapid Growth: Red Prana, and Yellow Prana
27. Reducing the Risk of Rejection of Transplanted Organs
28. Pranic Healing Applied in Surgery
29. Minor Surgery
30. Major Surgery
31. Food Poisoning
32. Insomnia
33. Disintegrating Deposits
34. Cysts
35. Cleansing the Internal Organs Technique
36. Cleansing the Solar Plexus Chakra Technique
37. Cleansing the Blood Technique
38. Fever
39. Master Healing Technique : Basic-Meng Mein Chakras Technique
41. Super Healing Technique
42. Pranic Healing Procedure
43. What to do when you are not sure

1. The Eleven Major Chakras have psychological functions
2. Thoughts and emotions produce emotional thought entities
3. The existence of the protective web
4. The existence of negative energy beings also called negative elementals
5. The use of pranic energy for the treatment of psychological ailments

Although the concept of thought entities, protective web and negative elementals are already taught in esoteric sciences, they were not linked and utilized in the field of psychological healing. Pranic Psychotherapy was developed by MCKS by using the five important concepts stated earlier and combining them with the techniques in Advanced Pranic Healing. Pranic Psychotherapy was also developed through experimentation and through the findings from clairvoyant observations.

It must be clearly stated that Pranic Psychotherapy had not been taught in other healing schools. Healing psychological ailments using pranic energies did not exist as a science prior to 1989 when the book, *Pranic Psychotherapy,* was first published.

*Pranic Psychotherapy by Master Choa Kok Sui has been published in at least sixteen languages, as of this date.*

## Eleven Major Chakras and their Psychological Functions

Each of the chakras have psychological functions. By treating the chakras, by inhibiting or activating the chakras, the behavior of a person can be positively modified, and psychologically healed.

| NAME OF CHAKRA | PSYCHOLOGICAL FUNCTIONS |
|---|---|
| 1. Basic Chakra | Instinct of Survival<br>Dynamic Activities |
| 2. Sex Chakra | Instinct of Procreation<br>Sexual Drive<br>Lower Creativity |
| 3. Navel Chakra | Instinct of Knowing |
| 4. Meng Mein Chakra | Regulates the upward flow of pranic energy from the basic chakra |
| 5. Spleen Chakra | Energizer |
| 6. Solar Plexus Chakra | Lower Emotion<br>Assertiveness<br>Center of Emotional Will for the masses |
| 7. Heart Chakra | Center for the higher emotions such as Love and Peace |

| | |
|---|---|
| 8. Throat Chakra | Concrete mental faculty<br>Higher Creativity |
| 9. Ajna Chakra | Abstract mental faculty<br>Directing Center<br>Higher type of Willpower |
| 10. Forehead Chakra | Center for Lower Intuitive Faculty<br>Center of Wisdom |
| 11. Crown Chakra | Center for Divine Love<br>Center for Higher Intuitive Faculty<br>Center for Illumination<br>Entry Point of Spiritual Energy |

## Thought Entities

Thinking and feeling produce energy beings which are called *thought forms* or emotional thought entities or thought entities for short. Calling them *thought entities* is more accurate because they are living beings. These thoughts and feelings are real and could affect and influence you and other people positively or negatively. When you think of something, you are producing a thought entity. If you think a positive thought, the thought will have a positive effect on you. Thinking negatively will naturally produce a negative effect.

When a person has had a traumatic experience, the traumatic energies produced are lodged in several chakras or energy centers which may, in the long run, manifest as stress or phobia. These traumatic energies have certain degrees of consciousness and are called *traumatic thought entities*. A phobia is nothing more than traumatic fear energy or phobia thought entities that are lodged in a certain chakra or chakras of the patient. Once the phobia thought entities or the fear energies are partially or completely removed from the chakras by the Pranic Healer, the patient will feel a definite improvement.

A traumatic experience may produce repeated thoughts of fear, poor self-esteem, insecurity, futility, and/ or indifference. Thinking and feeling negatively for a long period of time will produce negative thought entities with strong inhibiting effects, manifesting as severe depression.

The phobia thought entities are located in the congested areas of the solar plexus, throat, and crown chakras. Obsession and compulsion are also due to powerful thought entities lodged in the solar plexus, throat, and crown chakras.

## Protective Web and Negative Elementals

Located at the back of the chakra, near the surface of the body, is an "energy web". It is slightly smaller than the chakra by about one inch in diameter. This energy web is called *protective web* because it acts as a filter to protect the person from negative external influences.

When a person harbors negative thoughts or feelings or has negative habits, the protective web becomes cracked or punctured after a prolonged period of time. Since the person is filled with negative thoughts and emotions, he also attracts negative entities which enter through the holes or cracks in the protective web. This will make him do terrible things that he would not normally do. For instance, when a person is extremely angry, the protective web of certain chakras becomes ruptured. The moment anger is expressed, anger entities are attracted and they attach themselves to the person through the ruptured protective web.

If the psychological ailment is not very severe, then some of the protective webs are just cracked. In more serious cases, some protective webs are punctured and have big holes. This makes the patient susceptible to "psychic disturbances" or "intrusions" from negative energy entities or elementals. In Christian terms, these are called "bad spirits". The author prefers not to use the word "demon" because it is too harsh and does not give an accurate picture or impression on the nature of the problem. In the Holy Bible, there are many cases of patients with severe psychological ailments which were healed by exorcism or removal of negative elementals.

There are some beings that exist only with energy bodies whose consciousness is not substantially developed. These beings are called elementals and are encountered most often in people with psychological disorders. *They are energy parasites and they depend on negative energy for sustenance.* The chakras of a psychotic person may contain many negative elementals. To heal the person, the negative elementals have to be removed and disintegrated.

What is the difference between a thought entity and an elemental? A thought entity is an artificial being that you can create while an elemental is a naturally-occurring lower energy being in the invisible world.

These negative elementals are about one-third of an inch to several inches in size, depending upon their nature and their degree of influence over a person. They are able to influence the person through cracks or holes in the protective web. Although these negative elementals cause a lot of problems and disturbances in psychologically imbalanced patients, they are actually quite weak and can easily be destroyed by experienced Pranic Healers. These negative elementals are nothing more than etheric parasites. They can be easily destroyed by an act of the healer's will, and the use of the electric violet pranic energy.

When you are healing, the elementals cannot enter your body since you have protective webs. Therefore, there is no danger of contamination from the elementals. Besides, the protective web is made in such a way that, if there are any psychic intruders, it becomes automatically stronger and impenetrable.

The difference between a clairvoyant and a crazy person is a clairvoyant's protective web is quite thin and can easily be opened when the clairvoyant faculty is being used, and closed when it is not being used. It can be opened and closed subconsciously or intentionally. In other words, the protective web is just like a shutter that can be opened or closed at will by the clairvoyant. He has substantial mastery over his emotions, especially fear, and can see angels, fairies, and negative elementals without becoming psychologically imbalanced. On the other hand, a crazy person's protective web is punctured and the holes cannot be closed at will. The protective web is damaged and stays open permanently, thereby, making the person susceptible to attacks from negative entities. He is constantly influenced, bothered or tormented by negative thought entities, negative elementals, and negative disincarnate spirits. He sees ugly and scary things, or hears ugly voices.

These cracks or holes are caused by negative thinking, feeling and habits. Hallucinogenic chemicals destroy part of the protective web. The protective web of a person who takes hallucinogenic drugs like LSD or other harmful mood-altering drugs are destroyed and the person becomes psychologically imbalanced. When a person with no spiritual training uses a hallucinogenic substance or chemical, he is likely to have quite an unpleasant experience.

When a person is intensely angry, the protective webs of the solar plexus chakra, the ajna chakra and sometimes the crown chakra are ruptured. Intense anger attracts negative elementals of a very violent nature. They attach themselves to the angry person through the ruptured protective webs. The angry person then becomes temporarily possessed or insane and does terrible things that he will not normally do. How long these elementals will attach themselves to a person depends on the nature of the person. If he is the type who gets intensely angry quite often, then the insanity could become relatively permanent. These negative elementals feed on anger or need angry energy to survive and, therefore, will regularly incite or stimulate the person to anger.

## Removing the Negative Thought Entities and Negative Elementals

How, then, will you remove these negative thought entities and negative elementals lodged in the different chakras? Imagine that you are a clairvoyant and that a patient with a psychological ailment is in front of you. You are now looking at the dirty negative thoughts, entities and elementals. Instinctively, what would you do? You would reach out to them and try to sweep or pluck out the grayish thought entities and negative elementals just as you would the pieces of paper or dirt lying on the floor. You notice that the negative thought entities and negative elementals tend to resist. So you exert greater willpower to remove them. Exertion of willpower is done by just having a clear and steady intention. You will observe that a few come off but a substantial number still remains. So you apply more sweeping until the chakra is completely clean. This is exactly what the healer does and how Pranic Psychotherapy was developed.

If elementary sweeping is applied, it may require as much as 50 sweepings or more in order to clean thoroughly the chakra and its protective web, depending upon the skill of the healer and the severity of the ailment. It is necessary to have a basin of water with salt to properly dispose of the negative elementals and the negative thought entities.

A more advanced technique of removing these negative entities is to use electric violet pranic energy. Negative elementals and thought entities are easily overwhelmed and destroyed by electric violet pranic energy. In other words, electric violet pranic energy is anti-negative elementals and anti-negative thought entities. When electric violet pranic energy is used, the number of sweeping required is greatly reduced.

Sweeping has to be done slowly and gently, not too abruptly or willfully, because the chakra and its protective web can be damaged and this can adversely affect the patient's health.

## Sealing Chakras and Holes on the Protective Web

Cracks or holes on the protective web can be easily sealed by energizing with pranic energy. When elementary or intermediate energizing is used, the seal is not so durable and strong. A more advanced technique is to apply violet pranic energy which is more durable and can easily disintegrate negative elementals and negative thought entities. The use of violet pranic energy reduces energizing time, and the effect is also stronger and more lasting than by just using ordinary white pranic energy. Therefore, it requires fewer and less frequent pranic treatments. The seal is stronger and more durable compared to ordinary white pranic energy, and cannot be easily repenetrated by negative elementals. However, the seal created by the use of electric violet prana is even stronger and more durable than violet prana.

Flicking of the hand has to be done frequently when energizing in order to throw away the dirty energy. By energizing the affected chakra and the protective web, the cracks or punctures on the protective web are sealed. But there will be a relapse if the psychological ailment is of long-standing. Therefore, pranic treatments have to be repeated several times per week until the condition stabilizes. If the ailment is very severe, the treatments have to be repeated several times a day.

## Too Much Force or Will When Healing May Destroy the Protective Web

Avoid using too much force or will when healing psychologically imbalanced patients. Otherwise, the rate of absorption of the projected pranic energy is slower. The rate of healing, therefore, is also slower. The use of the will should be kept at a minimum level.

Energizing with too much will may also cause the protective web to rupture. You should also take your time when healing because too much energy will overwhelm the patient. When you energize a patient with compassion and loving kindness, the patient's body will be able to assimilate the projected energy faster, thereby resulting in a faster rate of healing. When pranic energy is impregnated with loving kindness, healing is much more rapid.

## Chakral and Auric Shields

Since there is a tendency for the patient to, again, rupture the protective web and attract negative elementals, it is advisable to create chakral shields for the affected chakras and to create auric shields to prevent negative elementals from psychologically reinfecting the patient.

When a patient is very ill, the doctor usually puts the patient in an intensive care unit (ICU). Since the patient has a very weak resistance, he can easily get infected or reinfected if the necessary precautions are not taken to protect him. This is why he has to be confined in a sterile, relatively germ-free environment.

In the same way, patients with severe psychological disorders should have a sterile psychic environment. If you think negatively of your patients, you unknowingly attack them psychically. This results in delayed recovery. Therefore, it is advisable to create chakral and auric shields. The shielding is for protection against reinvasion by negative elementals and negative thought entities from friends, relatives and counselors.

## Positive Thinking and Feeling

To hasten the healing process, it is important to instruct the patient to maintain a positive attitude - to think, feel and act positively. Daily positive affirmation is very useful. The healer should create a positive image of the patient, and encourage him to create and maintain a positive self-image or a positive image of what can be through daily positive self-affirmation or positive visualization.

## Integrated Approach in Pranic Psychotherapy

Pranic Psychotherapy is only intended to supplement psychological counseling or psychiatric treatment. Patients with serious psychological ailments must consult psychologists, clinical psychologists, or psychiatrists.

Pranic Psychotherapy should preferably be applied before giving counseling. This is to reduce counseling time. The patient has a tendency to subconsciously "unburden" or transfer the psychological diseased energy to the psychologist or psychiatrist, resulting in health problems after a certain period of time. By applying Pranic Psychotherapy first, this is minimized.

Note: This chapter has been extracted from Pranic Psychotherapy by Master Choa Kok Sui, with minor changes.

Chapter 13

# The Development of Pranic Crystal Healing



Pranic Crystal Healing was developed through many years of experimentations and through clairvoyant observations. The concepts, principles and techniques of Pranic Crystal Healing were formulated and developed by MCKS.

Pranic Crystal Healing was developed to reduce the degree of contamination from diseased energy when healing using the hands. Also, to enable the Pranic Healer to instantly increase their healing power by utilizing the properties of crystals.

*Pranic Crystal Healing* by MCKS was first published in 1996. By early 2006, it had been published in more than seventeen languages. It has to be clearly stated that prior to the publication of *Pranic Crystal Healing* by MCKS, healing using crystals was just an art and was in a primitive state.

## What is Pranic Crystal Healing?

Pranic Crystal Healing is basically using a crystal as an instrument in Pranic Healing.

## Three Essential Properties of Crystals

What are the three essential properties of a crystal?

1. Subtle Energy Condenser
2. Programmable
3. Chakral Activator

## Subtle Energy Condenser

A crystal is a subtle energy condenser. This means that it can absorb, store, project and focus subtle energies. In a certain sense, it is just like a rechargeable battery that can absorb, store and release electrical energy. Likewise, a crystal can absorb, store, project and focus pranic energy.

## Programmable

If you look at a natural crystal clairvoyantly, you can see small sparks of light inside. The sparks or points of light are sparks of consciousness. This is a very basic form of consciousness. Synthetic crystals have minimal sparks of consciousness and, as a result, are much inferior when compared to natural crystals.

A crystal does not have any will. Therefore, it follows instructions without resistance. Say, "Absorb pranic energy," and it absorbs pranic energy. Say, "Project pranic energy," and it projects pranic energy.

People and animals have consciousness and willpower. This is the reason why they may or may not follow your instructions. If you tell them to do something, they can resist. You can command an animal to do something but in some cases the animal will not obey you because it has willpower. Even plants have consciousness. They have also willpower but to a lesser degree.

As stated previously, crystals do not have willpower. Therefore, they will follow anything you want them to do. When programming a crystal, do not give too much instructions or ask it to do complicated things.

## Chakral Activator

A crystal is a chakral activator. In other words, it has an activating effect on the chakras. What do we mean by this? When a crystal is placed directly on a chakra, the chakra becomes activated. If you ask a clairvoyant to look at the chakra, it becomes bigger, rotates faster and has more energy. Not only does the crystal activate the chakra where it has been placed but it also activates other chakras, especially the lower ones.

Although crystals have an activating effect on the chakras and tend to make the aura stronger and bigger, they unfortunately tend to activate the lower chakras more than the higher chakras. Notice that the lower chakras are bigger compared to the upper chakras. This implies that patients with heart problems, hypertension or cancer should preferably not have big crystals in their room and should not wear them on their body.

## Four Basic Techniques in Processing and Utilizing a Crystal for Healing

There are four basic techniques used in processing and utilizing a crystal for healing:

1. *Cleansing* is removing dirty energies.
2. *Charging* is putting pranic energy into the crystal.
3. *Programming* is giving instruction to the crystal.
4. *Stabilizing* is done so that the absorbed pranic energy will stay longer in the crystal.

For more information, please read the book, *Pranic Crystal Healing* by MCKS. Materials for this chapter have been extracted from this book.

Note: Crystals include diamonds, other precious stones and semi-precious stones.

# Chapter 14

# The Development of Arhatic Yoga

In 1982 and for the next several years, Mang Mike and Mang Nenet clairvoyantly monitored MCKS when He was practicing Arhatic Yoga. They reported to Him the results of the meditation. It must be clearly stated that Mang Nenet and Mang Mike did not know and did not practice Arhatic Yoga. Even during and after Arhatic Yoga experiments, Mang Nenet did not practice Arhatic Yoga because he had his own spiritual practices taught to him by his own spiritual teacher.

In the case of Mang Mike, because of his physical condition (due to earlier strokes), it was not possible for his body to withstand the energies generated through the practice of Arhatic Yoga. Therefore, he did not practice Arhatic Yoga. Without practicing Arhatic Yoga it is not possible to understand it deeply.

*The practice of Arhatic Yoga was almost second nature to MCKS. He had been practicing the different levels of Arhatic Yoga in His past incarnations.*

*Before Arhatic Yoga was taught to the public, MCKS personally experimented using His Soul and His body as a "guinea pig" for many years. This was necessary in order to refine and readjust the Arhatic Yoga techniques, to insure that the yogic techniques are safe for disciples living in present modern conditions. In several instances MCKS' body became severely sick. This was necessary in order to understand the possible problems that might be encountered by the students and to develop solutions to correct those possible problems. The modern students of Arhatic Yoga are indeed very lucky.*

When Mang Nenet and Mang Mike were clairvoyantly monitoring MCKS during His Arhatic Yoga practice, they would ask MCKS what He was doing. MCKS had to explain to them the Arhatic techniques. It was because of this that Mang Nenet and Mang Mike began to understand the science of Arhatic Yoga.

## Arhatic Yoga Level One

Arhatic Yoga Level One is based on the following principles:

1. Each chakra has a spiritual or psychological function.

2. Each higher chakra has a lower corresponding chakra.

3. The higher chakra must be activated first before the lower chakra is activated.

4. The purpose for this is that the higher chakra with the higher spiritual or psychological function must control the lower chakra with the lower psychological function, just as the manager or supervisor must direct the workers.

5. If the lower chakras are activated first before the higher chakras, the higher chakras will not be in a position to control the lower nature of the person.

6. This spiritual technique is very different from techniques practiced in India, where the activation is started from the lower chakras moving up to the upper chakras. In Arhatic Yoga it is the higher chakras that are activated first, then the corresponding lower chakras.

7. The principle of activating the higher chakras first instead of the lower chakras is very important. If this instruction is not followed, spiritual disciples may encounter serious problems. The weaknesses of a disciple will be magnified and instead of spiritually progressing, the spiritual aspirant will retrogress.

8. This is the reason why in ancient times, the guru would insist that a student undergo many years of inner purification or character building before they were taught how to meditate.

## Arhatic Yoga Level Two

Activating the higher chakras and lower chakras is not enough. They must be closely linked or connected. Just as the supervisor or the manager must be closely connected with the workers, and the workers must be closely connected with the supervisors or managers.

The purpose of interconnecting the activated chakras is to become a better person spiritually, mentally, emotionally and physically.

Many spiritual aspirants have a misconception that the purpose of spiritual practice is just to achieve divine bliss, divine ecstasy and divine oneness.

*These are just partial benefits. The purpose of spiritual practices is to accelerate the evolutionary development of the soul so that the person can be of greater service to mankind and the planet Earth.*

The 12th chakra of an ordinary person clairvoyantly seen
as a point of light. The incarnated soul is lodged
in the 12th chakra which is one foot above the head.

* From Achieving Oneness with the Higher Soul by Master Choa Kok Sui.

The 12th chakra manifesting as a golden ball of flame
12 inches above the head of a Buddhist monk.
The 12th chakra is known as the Pentecostal fire
in the Christian tradition

* From Achieving Oneness with the Higher Soul by Master Choa Kok Sui.

Of what use is a high degree of intelligence or expansion of consciousness or the achievement of tremendous internal power if a large portion of humanity still wallows in ignorance and suffering? Of what use is a super cargo ship if it carries nothing inside? The purpose of Arhatic Yoga is to produce intelligent, compassionate, good hearted, powerful disciples who will become great divine servants.

To do this, it is necessary to eliminate pride, self conceitedness, and self delusions. A person with great pride will not become a great servant; he will make other people his servants.

## Arhatic Yoga Level Three

Arhatic Yoga Level Three deals with internal alchemy and the building of the spiritual bridge of light (antahkarana) and the development of the etheric golden body.

Arhatic Yoga Level Two is part of Level Three. In Arhatic Level Three, the lower chakras are activated first so that the physical body can withstand the greater downpour of spiritual energy.

## Arhatic Yoga Level Four

Arhatic Yoga Level Four involves the activation of the 12th chakra or the blooming of the golden lotus bud. This is done through character building, service and living the life of a good person. Spiritual practice is not just meditation. It is a way of life. This must be remembered by the spiritual aspirant and disciples. Before the experiments with MCKS,

Mang Mike and Mang Nenet did not know of the existence of the 12th chakra.

Activating the 12th chakra before its time will not produce good results. Activating the 12th chakra without proper preparation will result in disaster. Without thorough character building, the practice of Arhatic Yoga Level Four will be disastrous. The positive and negative qualities will be magnified to a very high degree. The weaknesses or vices will be magnified to such a high degree that it becomes uncontrollable in some instances and the disciple will become insane. This condition is very difficult to reverse.

The existence of the 12th chakra is hinted in the Bible, in the Book of Revelation (Chapter 21:2), where it is stated that "... there is a city with 12 gates". In the Book of Revelation, (Chapter 22:2), it states that "... there is a tree of life which bears 12 fruits..."

In India, it is stated that, "... the dancing Shiva (the incarnated soul) is located twelve half thumb lengths (or twelve inches) above the head". The partially activated 12th chakra in the Christian tradition is called the *Pentecostal fire.* In the Buddhist tradition the 12th chakra is shown as a *golden ball of fire* above the head of the monk. In Taoist yoga, the incarnated soul which is lodged in the 12th chakra, is called the *spiritual fetus.* The spiritual fetus is the state of development of the soul of a young disciple. In the case of the masses it is not yet even a fetus. It is just a point of light. In Sufi tradition, the incarnated soul, which is anchored in the 12th chakra, is called the *presence.*

For more information, please read the following books by MCKS:

1. *Achieving Oneness with the Higher Soul*
2. *Inner Teachings of Hinduism Revealed*
3. *Om Mani Padme Hum*
4. *The Spiritual Essence of Man*

## Arhatic Yoga Level Five

Both Mang Mike and Mang Nenet noted that something was coming out of the forehead of MCKS. This was, of course, on different occasions.

MCKS had to explain to them the technique. What is coming out is a vortex of energy from His forehead. This vortex of energy is called the *unicorn light*. There are different sizes of unicorn light. From the size of about 1 centimeter, in length, to several meters in length.

Sometimes, the spiritual teacher will appear in the inner world as a w*hite unicorn* with wings or a combination of *unicorn* and *pegasus,* the flying horse.

There are many spiritual beings in the inner world who have a fully mature unicorn light. They are the coworkers in the continuous creation in the universe.

## Arhatic Yoga Level Six and Seven

Arhatic Yoga Level Six and Level Seven are for arhatship and deal with the spiritual practices needed to become *arhats* or *paramahansa*. Arhatship is a state when the higher soul reaches a very high degree of development. The incarnated soul achieves an almost complete union with the higher soul. This is the ultimate in soul realization.

## Arhatic Yoga Level Eight and Higher

Arhatic Yoga Level Eight and Higher deal with God Realization and of this nothing can be said publicly. *These higher Arhatic levels have not been taught by MCKS to any of His senior disciples, because none of them are ready for these higher spiritual teachings.*

The way Arhatic Yoga levels have been categorized is different now than it was five to seven years ago. Five to seven years ago, the sublevels of Arhatic Yoga were categorized as separate Arhatic levels by themselves.

## Meditation on Twin Hearts

Meditation on Twin Hearts is a higher form of the Meditation on Loving Kindness, called *metta* in Buddhism. The purposes why this meditation was revealed to the public are:

1. To heal the planet. The loving energy generated can also be used to heal a small part of a city, a city, a state, or a country if done for a prolonged period of time by a sufficient number of people.

2. To increase the healing power of Pranic Healers. When practiced consistently for a long period

of time, this meditation will activate the crown chakra of the healer to a high degree. A highly developed crown chakra is necessary to produce rapid healing or even miraculous healing in many instances. The technique in Meditation on Twin Hearts is based on a small section of Arhatic Yoga Level Two.

3. Both Mang Mike and Mang Nenet noticed that during meditation, the crown of MCKS became very highly activated. It opened up like a big fiery golden lotus flower. They asked MCKS what he did. MCKS had to explain that to activate the crown chakra, it is necessary to activate the heart chakra first.

4. Without the ability to have compassion, mercy and love toward the people around you, how can you feel a certain degree of universal compassion and love for others, whom you do not even know?

## Procedure for Meditation on Twin Hearts

1. In Meditation on Twin Hearts, the heart chakra is activated first by blessing every person and every being with loving kindness through the heart chakra.

2. The crown chakra is activated by blessing the Earth, every person, every being through the crown chakra.

3. By blessing the Earth through the heart and crown chakras simultaneously.

4. The aura, the chakras and the different subtle bodies are further purified, by chanting the mantra Om.

5. Also, by chanting the mantra Om, the consciousness of the soul is raised to a higher frequency, thereby eventually enabling it to function in the higher world.

6. By meditating on the stillness between the two Om's. Through stillness, the soul is able to function in the higher inner world which has been prepared by the earlier steps.

## Arhatic Preparatory Level

After teaching several classes on Arhatic Level One, Two and Three, MCKS realized these spiritual aspirants were not like Him at all - when He was young.

Their knowledge and spiritual skill were very limited, if not near zero. It was necessary to develop a Preparatory Level for them so that they could gradually go up to the higher levels of Arhatic Yoga. The fundamentals of Arhatic Yoga had to be explicitly stated under the name, Five Pillars of Arhatic Yoga.

## Five Pillars of Arhatic Yoga

1. Devotion to the Supreme Being and Reverence to the Spiritual Teacher
2. Purifications
3. Meditations
4. Study
5. Service and Tithing

## Devotion to God, Reverence to Teacher

Devotion to God and Reverence to the Teacher are very important. Without devotion to God, or at least reverence to God and to the Spiritual Teacher, the practice of Arhatic Yoga would not be possible.

Reverence towards the Sat Guru or primary spiritual teacher is very important. The Sat Guru is like the electrical outlet for the blessing of God passing through the Great Ones. Without the divine blessing from God and the Great Ones, passing through the Sat Guru or the physical spiritual teacher, there is minimal divine guidance, minimal divine help, and minimal divine protection. To practice Arhatic Yoga under such conditions would be tantamount to physical and spiritual suicide.

*There is only one physical Sat Guru for Arhatic Yoga, that is MCKS. The rest of the senior disciples teaching Arhatic Yoga are Arhatic instructors.*

## Purification

Purification is divided into physical and inner purifications. In both instances, it is divided into do's and don'ts. In order for the physical and energy body to withstand greater amounts of spiritual and subtle energies flowing into the energy body and physical body, the following must be observed:

1. Proper Diet
   - No pork
   - Minimize meat
   - No fish without scales: eel and catfish

2. Abstinence
   - Smoking
   - Addictive and hallucinogenic drugs
   - Alcohol in moderation

3. Physical and Breathing Exercises Before Meditation

4. Physical Exercises After Meditation

Proper diet is very important. Pork meat and pork oil contain very dirty gross energy, which is completely incompatible with the system of an Arhatic yogi. The eating of pork meat or pork lard will cause the energy channels and chakras to become clogged up. This may manifest as chronic fatigue system, overheating of the body, chronic insomnia, skin rashes, severe hypertension, and other physical discomforts. In some instances it may even cause the yogi to have a stroke. Eating catfish or eel must also be avoided. They are not as dirty as pork, but are still dirty. Eating seafood with no scales should be avoided or substantially minimized. These kinds of foods are also dirty and are unhealthy for the body of an Arhatic yogi.

## Substances to be Avoided:

Addictive drugs, hallucinogenic drugs, smoking. Taking alcohol is permissible, but excessive alcoholic intake must be strictly avoided.

## Physical and Breathing Exercises

Doing Physical Exercises and Breathing Exercises are necessary to prepare the physical body and energy body for the greater downpour of spiritual energy and higher awakening of the kundalini energy.

It is also necessary to do physical exercises after the meditation. This is to get rid of old dirty energy and the excess energy generated by the meditation. It is important to avoid or minimize energy becoming stuck in the body.

## Inner Purification

Inner Purification or Character Building is an absolute necessity. Without inner purification or character building, the weaknesses of a person will become so magnified, that the person becomes worse instead of better. Character building is done through *Inner Reflection* and *Firm Resolution*. Inner reflection means reflecting on what one has done during the whole day. Firm resolution means to mentally erase the mistake done during the day, and to repeatedly imagine you are practicing right thoughts and emotion, right speech and right action. This has to be done repeatedly.

The key word is to *repeatedly* imagine. The question is why? It is part of ancient teachings that:

a. Repeated good thoughts will inevitably manifest as good actions.
b. Repeated good actions will eventually manifest as a virtue.

The Virtues are divided into Yang and Yin, or Do and Don't.

## The Five Virtues and the Golden Rule

### 1. Loving Kindness and Non-Injury

Loving Kindness

a. *Physical*
   - being helpful and charitable
   - being courteous
b. *Verbal*
   - being supportive and nurturing
   - being inspirational and instructive
   - being courteous
c. *Emotional and Mental*
   - being psychologically supportive and nurturing
   - blessing

Non-Injury

a. *Physical*

b. *Verbal*

   - harsh words, slanderous words or excessive verbal criticism

c. *Mental*

   - excessive mental criticism, enviousness

Balance Mercy with Severity

Balance Forgiveness with Justice

## 2. Generosity and Non-Stealing

Generosity

a. *Physical*

   - tithing
   - generosity
   - helpfulness

b. *Emotional*

   - warmness
   - nurturing
   - being supportive

c. *Mental*

   - teaching

d. *Spiritual*

   - blessing

Non-stealing

a. *Materially and financially*

b. *Affection*

c. *Credits and merits of others*

d. *Intellectual property: printed, audio and video work*

## 3. Objectivity (Honesty) and Non-Falsehood

Accurate Perception and Correct Expression

a. *Honesty*
   - avoid all unnecessary lies

b. *Self honesty and Non-conceitedness*

c. *Discernment and Prioritizing*

d. *Accurate Perception and Correct Expression*
   - scientific experiments and technology
   - proper management
   - calmness and skillfulness under crisis
   - foresight
   - wisdom

e. *Different Levels of Truth*
   - $1^{st}$ level - Tama
   - $2^{nd}$ level - Wasto
   - $3^{rd}$ level - Tumpak

Non-Falsehood

a. *Malicious deception or lies*

b. *Pride or conceitedness*

c. *Blind belief*

d. *Scientific and religious superstitions*

4. Moderation (Self-Mastery) and Non-Excessiveness

   Moderation

   a. *Work*
   b. *Recreation*
      - Fun
      - Food
      - Drinks
      - Rest
   c. *Sex*

5. Constancy of Aim and Effort and Non-Laziness

   a. *Regular practice of meditations at a definite time and place*
   b. *Regular schedule of studies and service*
   c. *Work responsibilities*
   d. *Family responsibilities*

6. Golden Rule and the Five Virtues

   a. *Five Virtues*
   b. *Yang Golden Rule*
   c. *Yin Golden Rule*

Character Building can be summarized by the Three Rules of Zoroaster:

1. Good Thought, including Good Emotion
2. Good Speech
3. Good Action

Character Building can also be summarized in the Teaching of Lord Buddha. In the first five of the Eight Noble Path:

Accurate Inner Perception

1. Right Viewpoint

Correct Expression

2. Right Thoughts
3. Right Speech
4. Right Action
5. Right Livelihood

In the Christian tradition character building is summarized by the Lord Jesus who said, "Do not murder. Do not commit adultery. Do not steal. Do not testify falsely. Honor your father and mother. Love your neighbor as you love yourself". (Matthew 19:8)

In the Hindu tradition, the practice of character building is called, Yama and Niyama. Yama corresponds to "Do" and Niyama corresponds to "Do Not".

## Spiritual Practices or Meditations

To accelerate the spiritual evolution of the soul, it is necessary to do meditation or spiritual practice regularly.

In Arhatic Yoga Preparatory Level there are four meditations which the spiritual aspirant must practice regularly.

1. Meditation on Twin Hearts
2. Meditation on the Blue Pearl
3. Arhatic Kundalini Meditation
4. Arhatic Dhyan

The purpose of Meditation on Twin Hearts is to develop the love aspect of the soul. In the Indian tradition, this is called Bhakti Yoga.

## Arhatic Kundalini Meditation

The purposes of practicing Arhatic Kundalini Meditation are:

1. To develop the will aspect of the soul.
2. To accelerate the evolution of the soul.
3. To accelerate the evolution of the physical body.

The evolution of the soul must be accompanied by the evolution of the physical body - just as the evolution of the computer software must be accompanied by the evolution of the computer hardware.

If the evolution of the soul is not accompanied by the evolution of the body, there will be a mismatch. The soul, in spite of becoming more evolved, will not be able to impress upon the physical brain many of the inner experiences. The soul will not be able to impress the insight derived through the use of *intuitive intelligence.* Intuitive intelligence in Buddhism is called buddhi chitta. This is intuitive intelligence which means *knowing* through direct inner perception - without having to study. The evolution of the body is important so that it can also withstand greater amounts of spiritual and kundalini energies flowing through the physical body. The cleansing and energizing effect of Arhatic Kundalini Yoga is very powerful. Because of this, a new Arhatic yogi should only do this mediation once or a maximum of twice a week. Doing this every day would cause severe hypertension. Another effect of Arhatic Kundalini Meditation is the cleansing of the energy channels, the chakras and the aura.

## Arhatic Dhyan

The purpose of Arhatic Dhyan is to develop the capacity for *prolonged awareness.* The word *Zen* is derived from the Chinese word, *Chan.* The Chinese word, Chan, is derived from the Indian word *Dhyan.* The word Dhyan means *prolonged awareness.* In many books on commentaries on Patanjali's Yoga Sutras, the word, Dhyan, has been mistranslated as prolonged concentration, which is incorrect.

**Blue Pearl**

The blue pearl is the seed of consciousness
or the mental permanent seed found in the crown chakra
and located in the pineal gland. By meditating on the blue pearl,
one can achieve greater oneness with the Higher Soul.

* From Achieving Oneness with the Higher Soul by Master Choa Kok Sui.

## Meditation on the Blue Pearl

To understand the purpose of Meditation on the Blue Pearl, one must first understand what the blue pearl is. The blue pearl is not the incarnated soul. The blue pearl is not the higher soul. The blue pearl* is the "terminal" for the higher soul. In Buddhism, the blue pearl is called the *blue disk*. In Sufism, the blue pearl is called the *essence*. In Christian tradition, the blue pearl is called the *eye of the needle*. (Matthew 19:24, Mark 10:25)

In the Bible, it is stated, "Let your eye be one and your body will be filled with light". (Matthew 6:22) The "eye" refers to the pineal gland. Within the pineal gland is "the eye of the needle", through which the camel or disciple can enter heaven. "Truly, Heaven is not here, there or everywhere. It is within you". (Luke 17:21)

The Meditation on the Blue Pearl should not be overpracticed. In some disciples, it may cause the body to become sick. It is analogous to an electrical wire that is subjected to too much power. It may overheat and melt.

The pineal gland is the *ark of covenant* within each one of us. This truth can be validated through prolonged practice of Meditation on the Blue Pearl.

What, exactly, is the blue pearl? Based on actual experience and based on ancient teachings, the blue pearl is actually a very minute particle of light - smaller than a hydrogen atom, smaller than a nucleus, smaller than an electron. It is smaller than anything scientists can imagine being small.

* The term blue pearl was probably first introduced to the west by Swami Muktananda.

The blue pearl in the inner teachings is called the *mental permanent seed.* The blue pearl is smaller than a grain of sand.

The glow of the blue pearl in an ordinary person is indeed smaller than a grain of sand. This is why in Christian tradition the blue pearl is called the "eye of the needle" and the soul of the disciple who practices moderation and non-excessiveness is called "the camel".

*The blue pearl is not used for healing because the spiritual energy is too intense or concentrated for the body of the patient. The 12th chakra is not used for healing because the spiritual energy is too strong or the spiritual voltage is too high for the patient's body which may be overwhelmed and make the patient's condition worse.*

By practicing Meditation on the Blue Pearl, one achieves the first stage of soul realization, where the disciple experiences he is not the body and that his body has disappeared. The disciple experiences his buddha nature. The disciple experiences the true nature of the atma or the soul which is basically that of spiritual light. The disciple or the yogi experiences his consciousness radiating in all directions. The soul or yogi experiences himself or herself as a being of light, traveling in all directions throughout a certain realm in the inner universe. Although this experience is wonderful, the bliss is intense, and the yogi experiences a certain degree of oneness, this experience occurs only in the lower mental world. This is only the experience of the incarnated soul not the Higher Soul.

On the second level of soul realization, the yogi or disciple experiences greater oneness with the Higher Soul. The disciple may experience a series of expansion of light followed by a dark void. The problem is the capacity of the brain to register these inner experiences and for the soul to comprehend these inner experiences.

The reader must eradicate pride, self delusion, if the reader wants to spiritually evolve rapidly. This is one of the most difficult weakness to remove and probably the last weakness to be eliminated.

Develop humility, humility, humility - and reverence to the Sat Guru. Without this spiritual development will be extremely slow. If a person does not have reverence toward the Sat Guru, how can they have reverence for God - whom they cannot see? How can they have reverence for God who is formless and cannot be seen?

## Arhatic Yoga and the Materialization of Negative Karma

When the spiritual disciple or yogi practices Arhatic Yoga, certain negative karma has to be worked out. Otherwise, spiritual progress is not possible. The higher the level of practice in Arhatic Yoga, the more ancient negative karma has to be processed. Where is the spiritual disciple going to get the "spiritual money" to pay for the karmic debts? This is done by *Service and Tithing*. To do service means to do good acts without any compensation. Tithing means to voluntarily donate 10% of one's income to the spiritual and charitable projects of the Sat Guru. It is by doing service and tithing that one generates good karma which can be used to "pay" or offset the disciple's ancient negative karma or karmic debts.

In order to avoid disrupting the life of the spiritual disciple or yogi, it is necessary to pace the teachings and practices of Arhatic Yoga. A spiritual aspirant should stay in the Preparatory Level for two years, or for a much longer period of time, and must put the teachings into practice. Spiritual development is not just *knowing* the teachings or techniques. It is *remembering* the teachings. It is putting them into *practice*. Ultimately, it is *mastering* the *teachings*. Knowing the teachings or spiritual techniques is nothing to be proud of.

An Arhatic yogi must stay in Arhatic Yoga Level One and Two for two years or more. Going rapidly through the different levels of Arhatic Yoga is sheer foolishness. Nothing good will come out of it.

An Arhatic yogi should stay in Level Three for two to three years or much longer, before proceeding to Level Four.

An Arhatic yogi in Level Four must practice this for two to three years or longer before applying for Level Five. An Arhatic yogi in Level Five must remain in Level Five until he has mastered Arhatic Yoga Preparatory Level and Arhatic Yoga Level One, Two, Three, Four and Five. This may take one or several incarnations. If a disciple computes the number of years it will take to reach Level Five, the disciple will compute it will take at least 10 years. Some disciples will say, "ten to twelve years - that is a long time". This is the perspective of a young or immature soul.

The student must realize it has taken hundreds of thousands or even millions of years for the soul to evolve to this level. Ten years to twenty years is nothing. Three to five incarnations is nothing to achieve *arhatship and mastership*. Be realistic in your aspirations. Be realistic in your spiritual objective.

Spiritually evolve rapidly not for the sake of pride or spiritual liberation. Accelerate your spiritual evolution so that you can be of greater service to others - so that you can become a better divine servant. That should be your primary purpose:

> *Be of service to others to become a humble servant of the Planetary God.*
> *To serve. To serve. To serve.*

## Maintaining the Purity of the Teachings

When the teaching is transmitted from the Sat Guru to the disciple, the distortion of the teachings, the degeneration of the teachings is inevitable, due to limited spiritual and intellectual capacity of the disciple. From the primary disciple to the secondary disciple to the tertiary disciple, more and more degeneration occurs. The teachings become more and more degenerated.

To maintain the purity of the teachings, the teachings have been inscribed into books by the physical Sat Guru. To maintain the purity of the teachings, study the books of the Sat Guru, not those by the primary disciples, secondary disciples, or tertiary disciples - for distortion is inevitable as the disciples try to comprehend the teachings. Follow these simple instructions and the teachings will remain pure for the next centuries and possibly even for the next several millenniums. Avoid mental and physical laziness. Read and study the teachings of the physical Sat Guru carefully and thoroughly. Put the teachings into practice.

## Using Discernment in Choosing A Spiritual Teacher

In this modern world, where information is so accessible through books and through the internet, almost anyone with doubtful qualification can become suddenly a "guru". This is what is happening in the so called New Age movement. Someone is channeling or receiving "inner transmission" from the Holy Masters, from the Green Tara, and who knows from what other sources.

The Sat Guru, like the disciples and like the masses, is still in the process of evolving and is not perfect. He, like the rest of the people is still working out certain weaknesses. One does not have to become "perfect" to be a guru or a Sat Guru. One just has to reach a certain level of development. The disciple must practice discernment. One method of discerning is by *scanning*.

Scanning:

1. Form the intention to scan the teacher.
2. Scan the spiritual energy radiating from the teacher.
3. Scan if there is sufficient spiritual energy.
4. Scan the size of the spiritual cord of the teacher.
5. Scan the size of the crown chakra of the teacher.
6. Scan for pride.
7. Scan for self delusion.
8. Scan for anger and hatred.
9. Scan for malicious intention.

Those who refuse to practice discernment, those who refuse to see, will be fooled.

Life is governed by the Law of Change, even the disciples of the Sat Guru will change, sometimes for better, sometimes for worse. Some may fall and degenerate. Always check and recheck. Do not just base your perception on reputation, for everything is subject to change.

Practice discernment, practice intelligent evaluation. From the fruits you shall know the tree.

1. Does the spiritual teacher inflame the disciple towards anger and hatred?

2. Does he or she encourage you to betray and to lie?

One must be on guard. A disciple who refuses to practice discernment, or who does not practice discernment is not reliable - is not trustworthy and therefore cannot be depended on to carry on the spiritual work.

## Validation of Inner Transmission

Receiving inner transmission is not that easy. The reader must understand "energy of like quality attracts like quality". A person of less spiritual development with a lot of character flaws will attract doubtful beings or pranksters in the *inner world.* By the time these pranksters are finished with the person, his or her life is in chaos resulting in multitudes of problems. The people who receive so called inner transmissions in the west, are called mediums. Some do channeling.

When MCKS was young, He was very cautious about the teachings derived from inner transmissions. He tried to validate them by using the following methods:

1. By trying to clarify and to understand the teachings, using mental intelligence and intuitive intelligence. Not every person has the mental capacity to understand what is being internally transmitted. *As a matter of fact, very few people have the capacity to understand the higher teachings even when they are orally transmitted.*

2. By dissecting or analyzing the teachings, and correlating them with what He had learned before.

3. By repeatedly experimenting with Arhatic Yoga on Himself and His body for many years.

4. By having the experiments clairvoyantly monitored by His spiritual guides without letting them know their findings were being cross checked.

5. Based on His understanding and experience, the Arhatic Yoga teachings were validated, refined and developed into their present state.

6. Arhatic Yoga has been revalidated through the countless spiritual experiences and the following positive effects on the Arhatic yogis:

   a. A much bigger spiritual cord
   b. A much bigger crown chakra and other chakras
   c. A much bigger aura
   d. And refinement of their character

7. This inner transformation has manifested in the transformation of their lives in terms of career, success, money and family relationships.

The process of validation and revalidation took more than twenty years and continues even up to now. Validation of inner transmission is not done in just days. It takes many years.

## Higher Clairvoyancy and Lower Clairvoyancy

Lower clairvoyancy uses the solar plexus chakra. Higher clairvoyancy uses the higher chakras. To be able to see clearly it is important to utilize the higher chakras for inner seeing and to have a very clean aura. *If the aura is dirty then the inner vision is worse than that of a person having cataracts.* In this case, the inner vision is distorted by the thought forms and negative emotions within the aura.

The auras of both those who practice higher and lower clairvoyancy are usually dirty unless they have practiced regularly to clean their auras. The auras of the lower clairvoyants in most cases are not sufficiently clean. Therefore, the findings of these lower clairvoyants are usually very unreliable. Although there are hundreds of thousands of clairvoyants, these people have not substantially contributed to the science of healing or to any sciences for the reasons stated above.

*There are very few clairvoyants who specialize in the anatomy of the energy body of a person.* There are very few clairvoyants who specialize in the anatomy of the energy body of the earth. Some of the future findings should preferably not be revealed publicly. History proves that scientific findings tend to be misused for destructive purposes.

What we call "clairvoyants" are usually psychic readers or clairvoyants who read for personal matters. Some of them are good but many of them are not that reliable. One has to use discernment. Just because the clairvoyant is right in one instance does not mean they will be right most of the time.

A clairvoyant consultant who is guided by the higher beings is probably 70% to 80% accurate, maybe even slightly higher. The reader must remember that what the future will be to a substantial degree is also dependent on individual decision.

In some instances, clairvoyant consultants may have cracks in their protective webs and may have a lot of pride. In these cases they attract pranksters or small negative beings - elementals from the inner world.

*Some of these pranksters may claim to be holy masters or arhats, the Lord Jesus, the Blessed Virgin Mary or other great spiritual beings. Such advices or readings create chaos in the lives of their clients. To give up one's intellectual faculty and free will or to blindly follow the advices of so called clairvoyant readers is not a smart thing to do.*

Practice discernment. Scan the following:

1. The spiritual energy and the spiritual cord of the clairvoyant
2. The degree of cleanliness or dirtiness of the aura of the clairvoyant
3. Guidance from the higher beings
4. Scan for the presence of pranksters or small negative beings who misguide
5. Scan for thought forms of preconceived ideas
6. Scan the skill of the clairvoyant reader

There are a few good clairvoyant readers. They are not that easy to find. They can be as accurate as 70% to 90%. Their accuracy also depends on their moods. If they are in the right mood then they are more accurate. If they are psychologically not stable, then the reading is not reliable. Some good clairvoyant readers are very sensitive. Therefore, their moods can easily change. This is not in all cases, just in some cases. Another issue that has to be considered is the interpretation of what has been seen. An example:

About five pages of printed material were given to a good clairvoyant reader to hold. She started to become dizzy. She said she saw the planets and the sun, that the energy was overwhelming, and she fell to the floor. She could not understand what she was seeing. Later, it was explained to this good clairvoyant reader that what she was sensing was the testimonial of an Arhatic yogi who had received a shaktipat or spiritual empowerment from MCKS - in order to clairvoyantly see the Great Spiritual Being within the sun. *Seeing is not necessarily understanding. Please remember this.*

## Authorized Arhatic Instructors

Arhatic Yoga must be learned under an authorized Arhatic instructor for the following reasons:

1. Purity of the Teachings and Techniques
2. Spiritual Empowerment

   Unless the Arhatic instructor is authorized, the students will not receive spiritual empowerment. Without spiritual empowerment, it is like a house with no electricity. Progress will be slow.

3. To insure that the Arhatic students will receive divine guidance, divine help and protection.

## Renegade Arhatic Instructors and Arhatic Yogis

*Authorization given to Arhatic instructors is not permanent due to the Law of Change. Sometimes Arhatic instructors progress, sometimes they retrogress. If they retrogress or degenerate, then their authorization is revoked. The renegade Arhatic instructors or Arhatic yogis are disconnected from the spiritual energy of the Sat Guru and the Arhatic group. Without this spiritual empowerment he or she becomes like a deflated balloon. Because of this, some of the students will be disappointed with them, because they no longer feel the same inspiration and/or the spiritual energy radiating from them. This is the karmic result of the sin of pride, the sin of ruthless ambition, and the sin of greed.*

The Sat Guru can only point to the right direction. The disciples must tread the spiritual path. The Sat Guru may teach about inner purification or character building but cannot force the disciple to practice it. This is the root of the problems. Practice and master inner purification or character building to insure your spiritual progress.

## The Great Vision

The target is to produce one Pranic Healer for every family. One Arhatic yogi for every one thousand people out of the present population of about seven billion people. The target is to produce seven million Arhatic yogis. Out of every ten Arhatic yogis one senior Arhatic yogi will be produced. A total of seven hundred thousand senior Arhatic yogis will be produced. Out of every one hundred senior Arhatic yogis the target is to produce one baby Arhat or seven thousand baby Arhats. Out of every hundred baby Arhats the target is to produce one fully matured Arhat or a great Arhat. A total of seventy fully mature Arhats or great Arhats. Out of the seventy great Arhats hopefully three Holy Masters or three Great Ones will be produced. If this can be done within one hundred fifty years time the world will change, be transformed and progress beyond recognition. If this objective can be accomplished, we can have heaven on earth.

Chapter 15

# Spreading the Teachings



MCKS established the Institute for Inner Studies, Incorporated in Quezon City, Philippines on 27 April 1987. In late 1987, the book, *The Ancient Science and Art of Pranic Healing* finally came out. The purpose of the Institute was to spread Pranic Healing, Arhatic Yoga, the inner teachings and practices globally.

The main purpose was to alleviate the suffering of the people by complementing allopathic medicine with Pranic Energy Healing. Modern Pranic Healing is not intended to replace allopathic medicine. *Patients are encouraged to receive proper medications and/or medical treatment.* It must be clearly stated that MCKS visits medical doctors and dentists regularly.

The World Pranic Healing Foundation was established on 23 July 1990. Its purpose was to spread Modern Pranic Healing in developing countries and in poorer areas. It had a humble beginning with only one table and a chair, shared by six staff members.

The World Pranic Healing Foundation is presently managed by Daniel Gorgonia, Daphne Bigcas and others. Through the support and help of some of the Pranic Healing graduates, the Institute for Inner Studies, Inc., and World Pranic Healing Foundation grew and expanded.

Hector Ramos, Faith Sawey, Hermie Corcuera, Daniel Gorgonia, and other Pranic Healing Instructors spread MCKS Pranic Healing all over the Philippines. The World Pranic Healing Foundation of the Philippines, Inc., was established in Pasig City on 13 May 2002.

## Indonesia

In 1989, Pranic Healing spread to Indonesia under the leadership of Mr. Indra Gunawan, a very capable executive, who is a kind and soft spoken person. He was a director or president of P.T. Gramedia Group of Companies, the biggest and most successful chain of bookstores throughout the whole of Indonesia. MCKS is very appreciative of the support and help from the executives of P.T. Gramedia.

On 26 October 1994, the Yayasan Prana Indonesia or the Indonesia Pranic Healing Foundation was formed. This was done through the effort of Mr. Indra Gunawan.

Hermie Corcuera of World Pranic Healing Foundation regularly goes to Indonesia to teach and to train the Indonesian Pranic Healing instructors. Through the dedicated effort of the Indonesian Pranic Healing instructors, MCKS Pranic Healing has spread all over Indonesia. It has been partly assimilated by the martial arts community in Indonesia.

## Asia

MCKS Pranic Healing also spread to Malaysia, Singapore, Hong Kong, Thailand, South Korea and China. Pranic Healing was brought to Thailand by Dr. Wannee Likhittam, a former dean of a graduate school of psychology.

In 1991, MCKS' book on Pranic Healing was translated and published in China.

In 2004, MCKS Pranic Healing was spread to Japan by Dr. Hazel Wardha of Australia. Dr. Hazel with the help of Dr. Masaru Emoto, a distinguished Japanese scientist and author of the famous book, *The Hidden Messages in Water,* organized MCKS Pranic Healing in Japan.

## India, Middle East and Africa

From the Philippines, MCKS Pranic Healing spread to India. A very kind Catholic priest named Fr. George Kolath brought Pranic Healing to Kerala, India in 1991. This was done with the help of a Catholic nun named Sister Eliza Kuppozhackel. The first Pranic Healing Foundation in India was established in Kerala by Fr. George and Sr. Eliza on 22 September 1991.

Before his involvement in Pranic Healing, Father George Kolath established and managed rehabilitation centers for drug addicts and alcoholics.

One of the students attending a Pranic Healing class was a devout Hindu business tycoon named Mr. C. Sundaram. He established the Indian Pranic Healing Foundation on 15 September 1993, in Bangalore.

Hector Ramos, Danny Gorgonia and other Pranic Healing instructors from the World Pranic Healing Foundation taught MCKS Pranic Healing all over India.

Later, on 30 January 1996, the All India Pranic Healing Foundation Trust was formed and later renamed the All India Yoga Vidya Pranic Healing Foundation Trust on 6 August 2003.

Through the guidance of the board of trustees from the various Pranic Healing Foundations and the dedicated effort of the Indian Pranic Healing instructors, MCKS Pranic Healing has been taught all over India.

From Bangalore, MCKS Pranic Healing spread all over India. There are now 17 Pranic Healing Foundations throughout India. These Pranic Healing Foundations are predominantly managed by volunteers. Men and women of *goodwill with the will to do good.*

Danny Gorgonia, Sriram Rajagopal, Hemal Shah and other Pranic Healing instructors spread Pranic Healing to the Middle East and Africa. Sushil and Ramani Joseph spread MCKS Pranic Healing to Sri Lanka and it was later continued by Sumi Lazar. Shakun Goyal spread MCKS Pranic Healing to Bhutan.

From India, MCKS Pranic Healing spread to the surrounding Indian sub-continent, to the Middle East and Africa. On the Indian Sub-Continent MCKS Pranic Healing went to Sri Lanka, Bangladesh, and Bhutan. In Africa, MCKS Pranic Healing spread to Nigeria, Kenya, South Africa, Mauritius, Togo, Benin and Ghana.

On 15 September 2004, the book entitled, *Inner Teachings of Hinduism Revealed* by Master Choa Kok Sui was finally published in India. This book explains the inner meanings of the teachings and practices in Hinduism.

## Europe

MCKS Pranic Healing spread to Germany in 1990. In 1994, an Indian and German couple named Sai and Ruth Choletti, learned MCKS Pranic Healing. Together with their instructors, they began actively spreading MCKS Pranic Healing throughout Germany.

MCKS Pranic Healing has also spread throughout Austria and Switzerland. Stefan Weiss, together with his Pranic Healing instructors, are actively spreading MCKS Pranic Healing throughout Switzerland.

In 1991, MCKS' Pranic Healing book was published in Italy. In 1992, MCKS Pranic Healing was brought to Italy by Roberto Zamperini. There are now five MCKS Pranic Healing Centers in Italy. The heads of these five centers are: Loretta and Leonardo Cigolini of Central Italy, Nadia Minussi of North Eastern Italy, Guiseppe Fratto of North Western Italy, Francesca Angrisano of Rome, and Maurizio Parmeggiani of Southern Italy. MCKS Pranic Healing has spread throughout Italy.

From Italy, a German scientist by the name of Dr. Rainer Krell spread Pranic Healing to Turkey, Bulgaria and the United Kingdom. Ana Maria Vargas, the wife of Dr. Rainer Krell spread Pranic Healing to Spain. Sonia Grassi of Brazil spread Pranic Healing to Portugal. Tor Frederick Karlsson, who at that time was residing in Italy, brought Pranic Healing to the Scandinavian countries. Hannele Johansson and Pekka Kaariainen are actively spreading the teachings in Finland, Sweden and Norway. Pranic Healing was spread to Denmark by a scientist from Costa Rica named Dr. Kirsten Visona. MCKS Pranic Healing has also spread to the Netherlands, Belgium, France, Cyprus and Greece.

MCKS Pranic Healing has spread also to Central and Eastern Europe, including Poland, Czech Republic, Hungary, Russia, Kazakhstan, Ukraine, Georgia, Romania, Croatia, Slovenia, Slovakia, Bosnia-Herzegovina and to the Baltic, including Latvia, and Lithuania. Charlotte Anderson coordinated and directed the spreading of MCKS Pranic Healing in Central and Eastern Europe.

In 2005, Dr. Hazel Wardha with the help of Lynne McTaggart, an award winning journalist and well known author of *The Field - The Quest for the Secret Force of the Universe*, organized MCKS Pranic Healing in England.

## Australia

In 1995, MCKS Pranic Healing spread to Australia. Dr. Ysaiah Ross, a distinguished law professor and author of 14 law books and Wendy McDonnell, a Hatha Yoga instructor, spread MCKS Pranic Healing in Sydney and New South Wales.

In 1998, Dr. Hazel Wardha spread Pranic Healing to Melbourne and Victoria. Dr. Hazel also spread Pranic Healing to New Zealand and Fiji.

Melaney Ryan and her instructors spread MCKS Pranic Healing in Perth and Western Australia, and in Darwin.

The Pranic Healing Foundation of Australia, New Zealand, and Oceania was established in 2005.

## U.S.A. and Canada

In 1993, Duncan and Marilee Gohen, and Maria Christina Castro brought MCKS Pranic Healing to Canada. MCKS Pranic Healing has been taught in British Colombia, Ontario, Quebec and throughout the whole of Canada. Some of the Canadian Pranic Healers are also deeply involved in charitable work.

In 1990, Stephen and Daphne Co established the American Institute for Asian Studies in California in the U.S.A. Stephen Co and his Pranic Healing instructors have spread MCKS Pranic Healing throughout the west coast, the Midwest and the South.

Later, the Center for Pranic Healing was established on the east coast by Dr. Glenn and Marilag Mendoza and some Pranic Healing instructors. MCKS Pranic Healing has spread throughout the east coast, including Florida and Puerto Rico.

*The Universal and Kabbalistic Chakral Meditation on the Lord's Prayer* was finally published in 2001. *The Meditation on the Lord's Prayer* has been taught in the

Philippines, in Canada, in U.S.A., in Latin America, and in Europe.

In 2003, the book, *The Spiritual Essence of Man* was published. This book deals with the inner meaning of the Tree of Life, which was mentioned in Genesis and in the Book of Revelation, in The Upanishads and in the Bhagavad Gita.

## Central and South America

In 1992, MCKS Pranic Healing spread to Sao Paulo and Rio de Janeiro in Brazil. Sandra Garabedian and Yara de Fleury Molen helped organize the first Pranic Healing class in Brazil. Through the dedicated effort of the Brazilian Pranic Healing instructors, MCKS Pranic Healing spread all over Brazil. From Brazil and Uruguay, MCKS Pranic Healing spread to Argentina.

From the Center for Pranic Healing in New Jersey, MCKS Pranic Healing spread to Central America and South America and the Caribbean. Later, Maria Christina Castro of Canada and Dr. Santiago Aviles Lee, M.D. of Colombia helped coordinate and spread MCKS Pranic Healing in these areas.

Through the dedicated effort of the Pranic Healing instructors of Central America, South America and the Caribbean, MCKS Pranic Healing spread to Central America: Mexico, Guatemala, El Salvador, Nicaragua, Honduras, Belize, Costa Rica, and Panama. In South America, it spread to Brazil, Argentina, Uruguay, Paraguay, Chile, Colombia, Venezuela, Ecuador, Peru, Bolivia and Guyana. In the Caribbean Region, MCKS Pranic Healing spread to Dominican Republic, Curacao, Aruba, Margarita, and Cuba.

Through the help and financial assistance of Pranic Healers, there are now more than 24 Pranic Healing Foundations, Associations and Centers in Central America, South America and the Caribbean. These organizations are managed mainly by dedicated volunteers.


## Acknowledgement

It would be too voluminous to include all of the names of the hundreds of board of trustees and directors, or the thousands of volunteers, supporters, and Pranic Healing instructors. To all of these people of *goodwill with the will to do good*, your dedicated service and kindness are recognized and deeply appreciated.

Chapter 16

# Practicing Compassion



Feeling compassion for the homeless, for the hungry, the poor and the sick is commendable. But feeling compassion for these unfortunate people is not enough. This must be followed by the *will to do good*. It must be followed by compassionate action.

## Planetary Peace Movement International

For there to be peace on earth, there must be first peace within. For there to be love on earth, the hatred within each person must be replaced with love first. For forgiveness to manifest externally, there must be forgiveness within each person. The external world is to a great extent a manifestation of our internal condition. In the prayer of St. Francis of Assisi, it begins with, "Lord God, make me an instrument of Your peace". For there to be peace on earth there must be peace within each one of us. "Where there is hatred, let me sow love", for a person to be able to sow love, a person must first plant love within himself or herself. "Where there is injury, pardon". For there to be peace, love and harmony, the seed of forgiveness must be first planted in each one of us.

Planetary Peace Movement was established with the purpose of spreading Meditation on Twin Hearts which is a higher form of Meditation on Loving Kindness. Through the daily practice of Meditation on Twin Hearts, the meditator is internally transformed and filled with peace, love and forgiveness. As the meditator internally transforms; the external environment, the people around him gradually transform. The external condition and the behavior of the people around us, to a substantial degree, is a reflection of our own internal condition. If there is peace, love and forgiveness within us; there will be peace, love and harmony around us. If there is pain, anger, hatred, constant criticism; there will be disharmony, discord, and even violence in one's surrounding.

Planetary Peace Movement was founded in the Philippines by MCKS and Charlotte Anderson in 1998. The Planetary Peace Movement Trust was started in India by

Chairperson Kombli Rajagopal in 1999. In the year 2005, Nalini Ramesh joined Kombli and has assisted in spreading the Meditation on Twin Hearts in India. More than 125,000 people in India, especially students, have been taught and practice Meditation on Twin Hearts also known as The Planetary Meditation for Peace. Marilette Liongson is the International Coordinator for Planetary Peace Movement International, which has now spread to 67 countries throughout the world.

## Feeding the Homeless

In 2001, MCKS and His students were in Santa Monica, California. He noticed there were many homeless people on the street and the night was cold. There was a strange feeling within Him. Together with His students, they decided to buy some hamburgers and distributed them to the homeless people.

Later, this activity of feeding the homeless people, became a regular organized activity. In January 2002, a non-profit organization was founded by Lindsay Hirsch and other Pranic Healers from Los Angeles, named Feed Your Soul. The purpose of this organization is to provide food for the homeless, and money to put the homeless people, *back on track* - to enable them to return to "normal" life. Very often what is required is only a small amount of money to pay for the two-month deposit required for their rent and some money to last these people for a month or two - while they look for a job - which will enable them to get off the street and get *back on track*.

On the east coast of the United States, the Pranic Healers call their organization, Friends in Need. Another non-profit organization founded by Scarlett Mendoza and a group of Pranic Healers from New York City.

## Feeding the Hungry Children in Colombia

While MCKS was teaching *Meditation on the Lord's Prayer* in Colombia, a Catholic Bishop narrated the predicament of children who eat only Monday to Friday, but do not eat anything on Saturday and Sunday. This statement was rather confusing. How can children have something to eat Monday to Friday and nothing on Saturday and Sunday? The Bishop explained when children go to school on Monday to Friday the local government provides funding for one meal - so the school children have food for one meal per day on Monday until Friday. MCKS was completely shocked that these children were so poor, that they had only one meal a day to eat during the week and that on Saturday and Sunday had nothing to eat. MCKS asked the Bishop how much money he needed per year to feed these poor children. Money was generated through donations and was given to the Bishop to provide daily meals for the children for one year.

This shocking incident began the feeding the hungry children in Colombia. In 2005, the Colombian feeding centers provided several hundred thousand free meals to hungry children and to adults.

## Feeding the Hungry in Brazil

In Brazil, some of the people living in the *favella* (in English, known as ghettos) are so poor, that the children do not have enough food to eat. The situation is not as bad as in the remote areas of Colombia. The Pranic Healers in Brazil founded a non-profit organization called, Pao Nosso which, in English, means our bread. This foundation distributes food to the families of some of the students in the favellas. The Brazilian Pranic Healers buy food in large volumes, have them repacked and distributed to the poor families on a monthly basis.

## Feeding the Hungry People in India

While MCKS was in India in August 2004, a Pranic Healing student narrated a story from a newspaper that due to a massive drought, there was a woman who literally starved to death in a certain village in India. The Indian Pranic Healers decided to form an organization called Food for the Hungry Foundation. Five Food for the Hungry Foundations have been established in India, namely in: Chennai, New Delhi, Calcutta, Mumbai and Hyderabad. Several hundred thousand meals per year were provided in the year 2005.

The various Food for the Hungry Foundations in India are managed by volunteers.

## Medical Assistance for Poor Patients

A foundation in India was established by Pranic Healers which also provides funds for medical treatments, including funding for cataract surgeries, heart surgeries, and other surgeries as well as medications to poor patients.

A similar foundation also carries out this important work in the Philippines.

## Assistance to Victims of Disasters

During the Gujarat earthquake in 2001, Pranic Healing graduates donated and volunteered to help the earthquake victims. During the tsunami disaster in 2004, Pranic Healing graduates both rich and poor, generously donated from India and other parts of the world, to the victims of this disasters. Fishing boats were donated to fishermen to provide them with livelihood. In 2005, when Mumbai was hit by a disastrous flood, again Pranic Healing graduates showed compassion by donating and volunteering to help the flood victims. Pranic Healers also donated to the victims of the Kashmir earthquake in Pakistan in 2005. The readers must understand that many of the Pranic Healing graduates in India earn less than $200-300 US per month.

American Pranic Healers donated to charitable organizations involved with assisting the victims of hurricane Katrina in 2005.

## Feeding The Hungry in the Philippines

Food for the Hungry Foundation in the Philippines, provides funding to priests and nuns to feed the hungry people in Metro Manila and the Visayas and Mindanao.

A story was narrated by one of the Pranic Healers about a poor family. The husband had left the wife and children. The mother, due to extreme poverty, watched one of her children literally starve to death. It is really shocking that such a heartbreaking event could occur in this modern time. This foundation also provides microfinancing with zero interest, enabling poor people to start small businesses. It is managed by volunteers.

## Zero Hunger Act

If each country would pass a law, allocating a very small percentage of the total budget of the national, state, and city government level, to feeding the hungry children and hungry people, then hunger could be almost completely eliminated globally. Passing this law is not difficult. All that is needed is to generate enough compassion and the will to do good. All that is needed is for the government in every country to pass the Zero Hunger Act.

## Acknowledgement

It would be too voluminous to include all of the names of the board of trustees and directors, of volunteers, supporters, and Pranic Healing instructors. To all of these people of goodwill and the will to do good, your dedicated service and kindness are recognized and deeply appreciated.

*"For I was hungry and you gave me food,*

*I was thirsty and you gave me drink.*

*Truly I tell you, inasmuch*

*as you have done it to one*

*of the least of these my brethren,*

*you did it to me."*

Matthew 25: 35,40

Chapter 17

# Experiences of the Disciples

## Embodiment of Generosity and Wisdom

My Teacher, MCKS, has always been the object of profound gratitude, deep respect, and reverential love for me.

My life with MCKS started 15 years ago, when Pranic Healing, likewise was just getting off the ground. I always wonder about how, almost single handedly, he managed to launch Pranic Healing from the headquarters in Quezon City, Philippines to the farthest ends of the earth in less than 20 years.

MCKS had a vision. He has a mission. And, he ably gives it life. The greatness of Pranic Healing as a human endeavor is fully and totally - MCKS.

MCKS is a personal teacher to me. Beyond the teachings in classes or in groups, I am always amazed at how he is personal in his teachings to anyone who asks or needs guidance. What delights me are those one word, one-statement, pearls-of-wisdom answers to questions to which one would normally expect to receive lengthy explanations.

One grasps the truth easily, perhaps not as rapidly, but effectively, as it comes from his lips. One realizes the magnitude of the wisdom of this special teacher. I cannot share all the wonderful megabytes of MCKS' wisdom because MCKS deals with each student according to his or her needs. How I wish everyone could be given a chance to know our dear teacher in this mode - accurate in perception, correct in expression and wonderfully succinct.

One other striking trait of MCKS' character is his generosity. He is a perfect example of generosity. I have seen him give from his own pocket many times any amount in order to help a person in the street, a student in financial need, a foundation in financial difficulty, or victims of life's tragedies. These situations also become an opportunity for him to teach us the virtue of generosity.

One evening, after a riot in Los Angeles, California, a group of students were following MCKS. Suddenly, a ruggedly dressed man appeared out of the darkness. Rapidly, he was able to cross between the students, in order to stand beside Master. All of the students backed off. MCKS remained calm - as he normally does. He scooped some money from his pocket and without counting, gave it to the man. The man, in an almost inaudible but respectful manner said, "Thank you, Master". This caught some students by surprise. When MCKS was asked how this seemingly unknown person could have called him "Master", he simply replied, "A lost student". The wonder of the teacher!

MCKS remembers almost perfectly past situations and the questions asked. One example that always makes me marvel whenever I remember, was a question asked in 1995. It was finally answered in 1998. Perhaps at the earlier date I was not ready to hear the answer. The answer, when it came, was given in ONE statement. It was so fantastic that it changed the whole perspective of an issue for me for a lifetime.

I am fortunately blessed, by Divine Providence, to have had a change in my career, in my life, and to have made preparations for the next life - led by a teacher like MCKS. To MCKS, my eternal gratitude. Thank God for Master Choa Kok Sui.

*A disciple from Canada*

## A Marriage Saved

Many years back, I had met a young woman, I remembered as being very sweet and loving. After years of not seeing each other we met again. She was full of hatred, anger and revenge towards her husband and mother-in-law. Lawyers were assisting the spouses to destroy each other's lives. Their children were deeply disturbed, aggressive and a disaster in school. The young woman decided to come to the next Pranic Healing course where she listened very attentively to the teachings on character building.

At the end of the course, she came to me and told me how she felt so much love flowing to her and realized that she should return her husband's nastiness with kindness and should integrate Master's teachings into her life.

Two years have passed since then. The broken marriage was saved. The couple is now treating each other with respect and tolerance. The children, who at that time needed psychiatric help, are now happy students. Thank you MCKS!!!

*A disciple from Germany*

## Inner Guidance from MCKS

In November of 1991, I was sent with another Pranic Healing instructor to teach Pranic Healing to school teachers, parents and students in the small town of a mountain province in the Philippines. Unfortunately, a strong typhoon reached this area. During the class, the school building where we were holding the class was shaking and the wind outside was howling. Despite the strong storm, the participants were eager and insisted that we finish the entire workshop.

The next day, the bus trips were cancelled due to damaged roads, landslides, and floods. We decided to walk to the nearest town, 12 hours away. There we could catch the bus to return to Manila. We sank into knee-deep mud as we were weighed down by our heavy back packs. We laid on the road to rest, drank rain water, and hiked over landslides and big boulders. We survived on nuts and chocolate bars bought from a small store.

It was already dark when we reached the next town. I was praying for divine protection while we were being frisked by a soldier before being allowed into the town. I had the name of our contact person on a piece of paper and was praying to find the right house. All doors were closed. Then there was a voice inside me saying, "Walk straight ahead and knock on the door of that house". I followed this guidance and was surprised to find the right house. We were given a small room in the basement. I made hot tea from the thick ginseng extract MCKS had given us and went to bed.

What happened next was one of the most magical and unforgettable experiences. I had a very vivid dream, I saw MCKS right in the middle of the room standing, or floating about one meter off the ground. My body was deeply asleep, but I was so aware of the light - which was in him and coming out of his body and his hands. He was smiling at us with his hands blessing us saying, "You are safe. You are blessed. You are divinely protected". He said those words with so much love, that I felt so happy! His body was radiating light all around the room. The next morning, even though my body was aching all over, I was feeling so light, happy, cheerful, and brand new. I realized that MCKS is a real Guru, a living Spiritual Teacher, and that he truly loves us and cares for us. I felt so lucky and so blessed.

Since that time, he is a living presence in my daily life. I always see his face. He is my best friend, disciplining father and loving mother, guide, constant companion and great inspiration. He is inner strength and love.

*A disciple from the Philippines and the U.S.A.*

## Inner Transformation

I would like to share my thoughts about MCKS, my Guru. MCKS is a Spiritual Teacher, but he is not an ordinary spiritual teacher. He is very special to me.

I first met MCKS in 1994 in New York City. *My first impression of him was that he looked like an ordinary man. He did not have the unusual garments that other gurus have. Instead, he was wearing a coat and a tie, like a businessman.*

Since then, I have been lucky enough to see him at least four to seven times every year. My impressions of him grew as I got to know him better. I realized that he is not just an ordinary man, but rather an extraordinary man, a Spiritual Guru in the real sense of the word. He is a good example of someone who has the balance of Intelligence, Love and Power - three aspects of a genuine and highly evolved spiritual teacher.

Intelligence. It takes a genius to synthesize teachings into a simple, easy to understand language that anybody can comprehend. This art of synthesis is MCKS' specialty. Every time I attend his workshops, I am always in awe of how well he explains different topics. His insights on spirituality are given in a very crystal-clear manner. Each time I review the teachings, I understand them more, and on different levels of consciousness. I can see how fast his mind works. His mind never stops improving the techniques he teaches. This is why his teachings are very dynamic.

Love. One has to experience being with MCKS to fully understand the sweetness of his loving energy. Bliss is the right word to describe the experience whenever blessings are given by him. MCKS has such a peaceful and loving demeanor that just by looking at him, one could feel a sense of stillness. He has a great amount of love for everyone. He touches the lives of every person he meets. I look at him as a father, an adviser, a friend and a Spiritual Guru, all in one.

Power. Not only have I observed how powerful he is as a healer, but I have experienced his healing as well. He has produced a lot of miraculous healings. His words alone can heal. He blesses our wishes and they come true. His energy is tremendous, but his real power comes from his humility. I have never seen anyone, with such intelligence and power, yet with so much humility. MCKS attributes everything he accomplishes to the Supreme God and to his teacher, Lord Mahaguruji Mei Ling. For me, that is REAL POWER. I have so much respect for him because of this valuable trait.

The most important impact of MCKS and his teachings on me, is how he has affected my whole family. I have three wonderful sons who are very fortunate to have learned

Arhatic Yoga. They have taken most of the courses with us and have applied many of them during the very early stages of their lives. *They all turned into fine adults, and practice the virtues and character building taught by MCKS.* Thus, I have nothing more to ask as a parent. All I have is so much gratitude for everything that MCKS has done for my entire family.

I see MCKS as an embodiment of his teachings, he practices what he teaches. As a disciple, I see the importance of spiritual growth. I feel confident that by following his example, I am following the right path. Here is a special man, and a Spiritual Teacher who is showing me the spiritual path. He gives me hope and aspirations.

I truly love him.

*A disciple from the U.S.A.*

## Blue Pearl, Kabbalistic Cross and Pegasus

Discernment. MCKS expects his disciples to practice discernment. After one very powerful meditation, he asked me, "What happened?" During the night, I meditated on his question, tapping into my scanning abilities and other faculties. The following day, I mentioned to him that the blessings he had given the group were so powerful that the 12th chakra of all the attendees were activated. He gave his usual neutral response and said, "Good. Good". I perceived this to be positive.

Like Socrates, MCKS during conversations with us, his disciples, questions, prods and dissects. His inevitable question is "What made you come to that conclusion?" This teaches me to be more aware, understand certain things, issues and experiences.

Meditation. I am so mental in my meditation, that I somehow wish I could experience some of the experiences shared by other people. I later realized that even my simple meditations are deep enough. The most memorable experiences I have with MCKS are inner experiences. I have very deep and profound meditations when I am around him. Since I first met him, I make it a point to meditate in his presence.

One time, before leaving for the airport, I woke up at 3:00 a.m. in order to meditate in a nearby garden, knowing that I was meditating within his aura. On another occasion, I remember during a meditation in Salzburg, Austria, I saw the blue pearl and the kabbalistic cross. I started shooting upward like a bright silvery light, ending in a very blissful state. In another meditation guided by MCKS, I remember riding a pegasus (the flying horse) and traveling in different places in the inner world. Just by thinking of a planetary realm, instantly I am there.

MCKS explained to me that the pegasus is not a physical creature. During meditation, sometimes the spiritual teacher will take on the shape of a pegasus or white flying horse, in order to guide the disciples to the different realms in the inner world. MCKS further explained that the students should make proper salutation before riding on the pegasus.

Synthesis. MCKS reaches into the deeper meanings of esoteric teachings. He takes them apart, analyzes them, validates and experiments on them, ultimately discovering secondary and tertiary meanings. He then shares the synthesized essence or seed of the meaning with his students. To him, truth is dynamic and one can experience and see the inner teachings, if one tries hard enough.

Students. He once said that having a powerful meditation technique is easy, but the technique should be safe for almost all students. MCKS is always concerned for the well-being and safety of his students.

MCKS has made a tremendous impact on my life. This deep and loving appreciation for MCKS and his teachings will remain with me for the rest of my life.

*A disciple from the U.S.A.*

## Parents' Marriage Saved by Meditation on Twin Hearts

In 1988, my parents were having big fights. I had just learned Meditation on Twin Hearts and had been having mystical experiences. I thought asking for blessings after the meditation would help them. One night, after one of their fights my father left our home. I went to my room and started doing Meditation on Twin Hearts. During the meditation, I kept visualizing my parents smiling, hugging and being affectionate with each other.

After sometime into the meditation, my mother who had been crying, ran to my room telling me she was scared. She narrated that while lying in bed, she felt somebody embracing her. When she opened her eyes, she saw a figure of my dad's body embracing her. His body was made of translucent or transparent light. She could see through his body and see the pillow and the bed cover! She thought she was seeing a ghost and ran out of her room!

I asked, "How did you feel when he was embracing you?" she said, "I felt good". She went back to her room feeling reassured. The next morning, my dad returned home. They had a long, peaceful talk.

Now it's been 17 years and my parents are still together, happily retired, enjoying their farm. Almost everyday after meditation I always pray and ask for blessing for them.

Deep and heartfelt gratitude to MCKS.

*A disciple from the Philippines and the U.S.A.*

## MCKS Pranic Healing and Arhatic Yoga Transformed my Life

In the year 2001, I found myself in a difficult situation. I was mixed up, and not sure any more, of what was right or wrong. I also had severe illnesses, as well as did some beloved people around me. I was also experiencing financial instability. For 13 years, I had been working as a medical doctor in my own medical office. My daily work was wearing me out. I had almost completely lost inner stillness, which is essential to my profession as a caring medical doctor.

Since attending my first Pranic Healing course, from the first day, everything began to change. I began to use Pranic Healing in my medical practice immediately and soon achieved stunning results. I was able to work 14 hours a day, 6 or 7 days a week, without feeling burned out or even stressed. Patients very often, wonder where all of this joy and energy come from. I am enjoying every moment of my life and learning from it. I am grateful for the divine mercy which has helped me to gradually overcome inner problems and external obstacles.

Later, I attended the Advanced Pranic Healing course and Arhatic Yoga. After some time, I was allowed to teach MCKS Pranic Healing. I now feel totally "on track" again and, what is more important, I am not afraid of challenges or difficulties anymore.

Pranic Healing and Arhatic Yoga transformed my professional and private life simultaneously. People often ask, whether I do not miss my private life, but this *is* my private life. Living according to my destiny, and following divine guidance, brings such joy and makes me realize that I am now on the proper path. I became aware of divine guidance and can follow it again. When I became actively involved in Pranic Healing I felt so touched and realized instantly, that Pranic Healing and Arhatic Yoga are very important in my life. They are tools to develop myself. It is now up to me to pass the teachings on to others.

How can we develop? How can we recognise the meaning of our lives? These are the oldest questions. Many philosophers, medical doctors, healers, scientists, and religions have tried to find answers to these questions. Through the teachings of our beloved Grandmaster, through his blessings and support - I was shown the way. The path is toward spiritual growth, physical health and happiness. It is the path to soul mastery.

*A disciple from Germany*

## Conquering Fear

This story starts with my husband because it began with him. He was a very stressed-out bank executive, who was trying to find a user-friendly way to destress himself without the use of alcohol or drugs. He had tried different types of meditation, physical exercise and yoga, but none of these gave him what he was looking for. He was looking for something that would give him inner peace while still allowing him to maintain his practicality and effectiveness in his job.

One day, he saw Arhatic Yoga advertised in the newspaper. He thought it was another type of physical exercise and wanted to try it. He went to the Institute for Inner Studies and found out that Arhatic Yoga is an advanced form of meditation. He was asked to attend a class in Pranic Healing in order to understand the energy body. Even though he did not want to become a healer, it was necessary for him to take this 2-day course. As a requirement of the class, he needed to submit healing cases. Our two children were asthmatic, and our housemaids, driver and security guards had various aches and pains. I had a very low immune system and would easily catch any "infectious bug" in the air. After only one treatment, our children no longer had regular asthmatic attacks and the maids were pain free and very happy. The driver no longer had chronic back pain, the night security guard could stay awake at his post, and my doctor was very happy because at last I was responding to the medical treatment. But most especially, I became curious about Pranic Healing and Arhatic Yoga because I noticed a remarkable change in my husband. He had become less temperamental, more considerate and softer in his interactions with our family.

My husband was very leery about my meeting MCKS and others from the Institute for Inner Studies, his new friends, because I usually did not care for his unconventional friends. On our first meeting, we attended a picnic. MCKS sat down and talked about putting up the World Pranic Healing Foundation. I was very impressed about how intelligent, grounded, kind and normal these spiritual students appeared to be. They were all professional people with whom I could easily relate. The other thing common about them is that they were interested in developing themselves spiritually.

Some time later, I took Pranic Healing. During class, I was very impressed with the way the instructor presented the material. I had thought it would be mysterious. Instead, I found it very practical, understandable, and immediately sensed the power and depth behind the simplicity. I was also impressed that when there would be a negative experience, the Pranic Healers' first reaction was to bless. This compassionate response was unfamiliar to me at that time. Now, I attribute this response to be a direct result of knowledge of Pranic Healing, and the regular practice of Meditation on Twin Hearts.

During the class, we did the Meditation on Twin Hearts after which I got a major migraine headache for the first time. The instructor asked me if I smoked and I said yes, two packs a day, I was then told this pain could be a normal side effect for a smoker. The second day, I wished I could stop smoking so that I could experience what my classmates were experiencing. Then, the class ended and two weeks later my maid asked me what I would like her to do with all of the cigarettes in the house. They had been lying around for two weeks and she thought they must be stale. Only then did I realize that I had not smoked for two weeks and had not even had a desire to smoke since attending the class. I was very impressed at the wish-fulfilling aspect of Meditation on Twin Hearts.

What really kept me going, is that something was improving in my relationship with my husband and our marriage.

Because of the blessing part of Meditation on Twin Hearts, other changes occurred. One day, I realized that I was no longer reacting emotionally to people and events; instinctive reactions were now primarily mental in nature. That is when I realized the practice of blessings worked. This change took about 3 to 4 months.

The week I was scheduled to take Arhatic Yoga, my father-in-law died in his sleep. Funeral arrangements made it necessary for us to sit long hours, even into the night, because it is part of our cultural tradition to sit with the body - a wake. Additionally, we had to bring my seriously ill mother-in-law to our home from the hospital. Then, her nurse took a leave and did not return. On that same day, our maids took a day off and did not return either.

My husband and I were left to attend to the traditional wake and at the same time, take care of his bed-ridden mother. By the second day, he finally asked MCKS to do a healing for her.

Master kindly made time, came to our house and did the healing on her before the Arhatic class started. That night, she too, died in her sleep - with a smile on her face. Her smiling face was amazing because she was in constant severe pain for the last 10 years and did not smile because of it. This healing from Master, I felt was a great blessing.

The Arhatic Yoga class was given by MCKS on 5 consecutive nights. Every evening, after class, Master and some of the students would come to the funeral chapel and they would continue to discuss spiritual lessons. In the flower-laden chapel, there was my mother-in-law in the coffin, and my father-in-law's ashes in an urn beside her body and a lively Arhatic class extension.

That made me feel that MCKS and the Arhatic Yoga community became our spiritual family.

In 1995, we went to China with MCKS and three other friends. It was a very important event for me. Since childhood, I would get severe air sickness from sheer terror. After this trip, my body would never become air sick again.

During this trip, when we would start complaining of tiredness while climbing the sacred mountains on foot for many hours, MCKS would say, "Look, one day we can look back and say we can remember this and be proud that we have achieved something not many people have tried to do". Reaching the peak of the sacred mountains, I began to feel proud of myself and to appreciate the spiritual value of the simplest tasks and instructions. MCKS continues to inspire me to develop inner strength and courage.

One time, MCKS was teaching us a certain meditation technique, but when I started to experience myself being sucked into the crown chakra, I suddenly opened my eyes and stopped my meditation because I was afraid. I had never experienced that before. Master asked me why I had opened my eyes and why I had stopped meditating. I told him I was afraid that I would get lost in the inner world, because I easily get lost even just in Makati City. He calmly said,

"Why are you afraid? I am here. I will teach you". With this assurance, I became braver and was no longer afraid to practice meditation. This was a real accomplishment for me because previously, I had been generally afraid of everything esoteric.

On another occasion, Master said, "Energy is neutral". This realization was another important step for me in not being afraid, all is just energy.

One time, I had a dream that I had died. I was outside my body and was looking for the guide I had been told you would meet when you die. I was looking for the light at the end of the tunnel that I was told I would see. But I did not see any of those things.

Instead, I was in a void. I started to shout for someone to come but there was no one. There was only me. Then, I sensed the presence of a being who, without words, asked, "What have you done with your life?" Customarily, I started to make excuses. I couldn't do anything because my husband, my parents, my situation, etc. was stopping me. I looked around for someone to blame but I couldn't find anyone there but me. Then, the thought finally hit me - I was all alone in this space.

I realized then that it was not other people or things that are in my way. It was just, that I never really did anything. After this, I got sick for two weeks. Then, I went to see Master and said, "Thank you very much for teaching us to learn to be better people. I'm very, very grateful".

Later, he called me aside and asked me to handle a project, but I told him no; that someone else would be better at it, and that I didn't really have time. He replied, "You keep saying no. You say you are grateful for learning this and that, but when the Teacher calls you to practice, you say, 'Wait I'm busy, wait it's raining, wait I don't have the time'." I realized that this was actually what I had been doing all my life. And so, with the proper attitude and purpose, I decided to say, "Yes, thank you," and to constantly remind myself to practice the Teachings.

At the first Arhatic Yoga Retreat which was held in Anilao, Batangas, Master was teaching, us for the first time, the practice of the Meditation on the Soul. It was a pretty intense meditation and at that time, the 12th chakra was not being discussed. After the meditation, everybody was sitting very quietly and Master asked a question, but no one would give him an answer. He began calling out names but each one was making excuses. Finally, he called on my husband who was sitting on a narrow bench beside me. My husband responded, "Wait Master, I will ask my soul". Almost instantly, he fell off the bench backwards. His face and body were so red and very hot. Later, my husband related that he felt as though a big lightning bolt had literally hit him on the head and knocked him off the bench. This taught me *never* to make jokes about the soul. *Spiritual energy is real.* It is subtle. When focused and directed it can move dense matter.

Thanks to MCKS' presence, the Teachings embodied in Pranic Healing and Arhatic Yoga, my relationship with myself and with my husband is growing deeper and multi-dimensional. We are much happier.

*A disciple from the Philippines*

## Life Became Amazing

When we met MCKS in November 1994, we were at a turning point in our lives. We had been married nearly a year. I had lost my job as an agricultural engineer on a horticulture farm. My husband had recently moved to Germany. He was in the process of establishing his yoga school in a small town near Bremen, Germany. With the support of my parents and subsidies from the unemployment insurance, we were just managing to get by financially. I had been working as a massage therapist.

We attended the MCKS Pranic Healing course. During the break on Saturday, my husband introduced himself as a yoga teacher and MCKS invited us for lunch. He asked my husband, "How about teaching Pranic Healing in Germany?" My husband responded, "With your blessings, Master, why not?"

At that time, I had absolutely no clue what impact this would have on our lives. My husband gave his first MCKS Pranic Healing course in Bremen in May 1995. From that moment, events just started following rapidly one after another.

In summer 1996, we moved to Munich. We used our living room as classroom and my husband began traveling all over Germany to teach MCKS Pranic Healing Workshops.

Today, 10 years later, we are busier than ever with Pranic Healing. It has virtually become the center of our lives. The organization has grown. Now, we have 70 Sub-Licensees, 500 members in our Pranic Healers' Association, and thousands of graduates of MCKS Pranic Healing courses.

We have our own house with garden and two cars. We are very thankful to MCKS, for his blessings, and for being able to live very comfortably.

This is the obvious part. More important is the invisible part which is much more difficult to describe. The transformation began with Arhatic Yoga Prep in 1996. Only then I started realizing how lucky I was, to have been accepted by MCKS as a disciple. Slowly, after many confusions and doubts, I accepted MCKS Pranic Healing and the works of MCKS as my purpose in life, as my destiny.

I have gained inner peace, joy, love and bliss through the regular practice of Arhatic Yoga. It is not to mention a tremendous improvement in physical health, the cure of my allergies and severe asthma through MCKS Pranic Healing.

But the most amazing of all are the experiences I have had during the workshops of MCKS. Each time, it is like a quantum leap into a new dimension of indescribable bliss and joy, a new dimension of sensitivity and healing power, and of understanding, inner peace and enlightenment.

It is just impossible to describe the intensity of my gratitude and love. Can we ask for anything more in life?

*Two disciples from Germany*

## The Miraculous Effects of MCKS' Teachings

In the early years of my involvement with MCKS' organization, I was amazed by the fantastic results of Pranic

Healing. Patients were getting healed of their ailments and of serious life threatening diseases. Reports of their getting healed always struck me as something fantastic or miraculous.

Actually, seeing some people getting healed in front of my very eyes, whether by MCKS or by ordinary Pranic Healers, always amazed me.

After a while, when I kept hearing so many of these reports, I began to expect that healing is "supposed to happen" and the amazement diminished. Now, I sometimes feel amazed when someone doesn't heal.

Recently, while talking with another instructor, we discussed that the miracle of Pranic Healing is not that the patient gets healed. Pranic Healing happens because it follows certain scientific laws. The amazement and the excitement no longer come from hearing about these healing results. I think the miracles, the real miracles, are in seeing how people's lives have changed because of the introduction of MCKS' Pranic Healing and Arhatic Yoga into their lives.

I hear about people talking about how the teachings changed their lives and about how their relationships improved dramatically. Their businesses have grown and prospered tremendously. Their personalities have evolved to an extent that they can say that they are better people now.

*Most of these people have never personally seen or met MCKS. Some of them probably never will. But when they talk about him, they talk as if he is an integral part of their lives.* Some of them have not even read all of his books, but all of them have heard his voice in the recorded meditation and have felt the "energy" during the meditations.

The common denominator is seeing the faces of the students, instructors, and organizers change. That is the real miracle of the Teachings of MCKS. People change and their lives are transformed.

When I see a person over a period of four or five years, I observe them change so much, that by the fifth year, I wonder if this is really the same person I met five years ago.

I have seen families of Arhatic Yogis do their physical and breathing exercises together, like it is part of their daily routine. I wonder if this isn't going on all over the world. This is a miracle.

I think that when I teach any of MCKS' courses it validates some of the Teachings of MCKS. I am referring to his saying, "The more you teach, the more you learn".

Naturally, I follow the Instructor's Manuals of MCKS' Teachings exactly. Sometimes during the courses, when I am teaching, I hear words coming out of my mouth and I wonder where they've come from. During classes the ideas just pour out when I am talking. I wonder how I knew of those things. I feel like the observer, observing my physical body and my mind saying words, but they do not come out of my conscious memory, as the words that are outside of my experience. I view this to be a manifestation of the blessings of the Teacher, as this flow of information is continuous throughout the teaching process. This kind of information generally comes in response to the difficult questions from the students. I would initially think about how to respond, then the flow just begins and the answers come.

When these things happen, I realize that I have been a participant in a glorious spiritual process, involving the transference of ideas and energies. This experience makes me feel like I am doing something worthwhile with my life, for my spiritual growth.

As the observer, I realize that as we practice, our perceptions of the world change, our values change, and that what is really necessary, is for us to *internalize* the teachings of MCKS. We really must practice the techniques we have been given. In doing so, the entire world transforms before our eyes.

*A disciple from the Philippines*

## Healing a Drug Addict

When I was young, I used to dream of a very special man who does not speak Tagalog. I also dreamed I would be doing something that was not exactly ordinary.

This was my first job. I was referred to MCKS' office by my school, to work as a stenographer to transcribe a book he was writing. I was given an appointment at 10:30 a.m., but I did not arrive until 1:30 p.m. because I just kept getting lost.

MCKS' office was under renovation. The office was very dusty and extremely messy. There were lots of laborers around. Here I was, all dressed up for my interview, having to walk around hollow blocks and scaffolding, in order to enter the building. I wanted to back out.

The first man I saw in the office was wearing a suit and I thought that he would be the one who would interview me. But then there was another man at the side, who had eyes that seemed to look through you. I was never interviewed. I was only asked three questions. What's your name, where do I live, and how much salary do you want? I was accepted and they requested me to start immediately.

It was difficult for me. I had to look for so many words that were not in the dictionary. I only became convinced about the existence of pranic energy after I took the Pranic Healing course with MCKS. When he asked us to look clairvoyantly at one of the nurses, I was able to see the crown chakra. During the Meditation on Twin Hearts I was able to leave my body. From that time on, I started having out of body experiences. Whenever I would close my eyes, I would enter another world, the inner world.

I started to develop my other psychic faculties. When I could not see an aura visually, I was able to sense or intuit the color, the size, or what was wrong in the aura and more or less the quality of the character of the person. Later, I would generally find that the perceptions were correct.

In relation to the work and my life, in many instances, I could see what would happen in the future. For example, I knew that at the age of 30, I would be traveling all over the world with a spiritual purpose. I could not imagine why this would happen. I am not a Pranic Healing instructor and therefore did not think, I could not expect to do that kind of traveling; but this vision came true.

The most important thing MCKS taught me is more on deepening my faith. He also taught me that I can change my destiny and that my life is in my hands. I knew that I could become a special and unique person in my own way.

## Guided Transferred Clairvoyancy

*MCKS touched my body and I was able to see Samuel's health rays in 3-D. The vision was very clear, and they looked slightly thicker than that of a fine strand of hair. Later, MCKS activated and guided my clairvoyancy again. I saw them looking like luminous brass coming toward me.*

Then, MCKS asked me to look at Samuel's blue pearl, so I began to look at the pineal gland. I saw a small bluish violet marble. Then, MCKS asked me to look at this blue marble from the crown chakra.

When my clairvoyant faculty was activated further, the blue marble appeared bigger. *With the guided transferred clairvoyance, the vision of the blue pearl became much clearer, as though looking at an object with the physical eyes open.*

I requested to see something about the universe. MCKS said the solar system would be good enough. I saw the sun and the planets. They were like pulsating or "dancing" to the cosmic music which was soothing and pleasant. *The sun was rhythmically breathing, as though it was alive. There was deep peace and bliss.*

In the third experiment, he asked me if I would like to see the sun as a golden lotus flower. I tried but did not see the spiritual golden lotus flower. What I saw was *everything was gold and a huge, powerful Being interpenetrating the sun. I was stunned and awed by the spiritual experience.*

Experience With Pranic Psychotherapy

I received a call from my sister-in-law complaining that my brother was addicted to a form of synthetic cocaine. He had lost his job, was gambling and chasing after women.

His mind was cloudy and no longer rational. We could not talk "sense" into him anymore.

My sister-in-law sent me a photograph of my brother and his friends. I made an agreement with her, that she would call me when my brother was about to take the addictive drug.

Then, I would do Distant Pranic Psychotherapy on my brother and his entire group of friends - who were also drug addicts, as well as the room where they had their drug sessions.

She reported to me that the group would usually stay in the room for a long period, but when Pranic Psychotherapy was applied they would instead disperse rapidly. We continued the Pranic Psychotherapy for almost a month.

Then, he awakened one day and said he had no more desire to take the addictive drugs. He stopped smoking, gambling and chasing women. According to my sister-in-law, up to now, he never returned to those negative habits.

Before I met MCKS 17 years ago, my life and that of my family was financially very difficult. I was living a very simple ordinary life. After I met MCKS and began practicing his teachings, my life became much better. I was able to accomplish many things. Not only my life, but also my family's life changed materially, financially and spiritually.

MCKS taught me to be a good person - to take care of my parents, my brothers, sisters and relatives, to practice the virtues, to do service, and to do tithing for charitable and spiritual purposes every month. Now, I own a house, a car and have savings.

*A disciple from the Philippines*

## Inspired By My Sat Guru

My first contact with MCKS was in New Delhi in 1998. I received a shaktipat as he was departing after conducting a well attended lecture and demonstration at the Grand Hyatt Hotel ballroom.

MCKS inspired me from the very first day when I witnessed him performing miracles through Pranic Healing. I recalled the words of the Lord Christ, "What I can do, you too can do, and more". In front of my eyes, MCKS was demonstrating this prophecy of the Lord Christ. During those inspiring moments I thought to myself that if Guruji could fulfill this prophecy, we could all fulfill the prophecy - if we practice his teachings diligently. I resolved to work towards this goal, through the practice of Arhatic Yoga.

MCKS' loving kindness, care and consideration towards our family have been continuous. His healings have been powerful and magnificent. Whenever he has given me a healing I have felt myself turning instantly into a *pillar of light*, a most enlightening experience. He has created many cherished and happy memories for me, personally. I have had the rare privilege of being his house guest on many occasions and savoured his special and warm hospitality.

One memorable trip that we took with him was to the Valley of Flowers in the Himalayan foothills in 2003. We traveled upwards into the high mountains on army horses. For 14 kilometers, we remained with our hearts thudding with fear as we passed over the dangerous terrain. Traversing the last 7 steep kilometers, to the Valley of Flowers, we had to go on foot. Some of us wished to give up and return back to our base camp, but MCKS said that, "we should finish what we start". So we continued upward with him, chanting Om Nama Shivaya and the Gayatri Mantra to keep our spirits up. Finally, we reached the Valley of Flowers.

I look up to my sat guru, and observe, and attempt to emulate his great example of selfless service to humanity and his tenacity of will, and his dedication to the fulfillment of the divine plan for this planet.

I can honestly say that I owe my life to MCKS, because it was Pranic Healing that saved me from falling into the dark crevasse of rejection of life itself, when we lost our son. I am happy, inspired and filled with a divine purpose to spread MCKS Pranic Healing in Australia and in other countries. I am inspired to help humanity by alleviating their suffering through spreading MCKS' Teachings.

Due to the hard work that MCKS puts into spreading the love and light of Pranic Healing around the world, many lives have been enriched and saved.

God bless our Sat Guru with a long, happy, healthy, peaceful and prosperous life.

*A disciple from Australia*

## Blinding Ball of Light

I started as a very confused youth with no direction in life. I had no inner peace and was emotionally frustrated with life.

When my wife had a fourteen-foot fall and broke her hip bone, a double compound fracture, the doctor said it would take 3 months before she could place the slightest weight on her leg.

Fortunately, someone recommended attending a Pranic Healing workshop. I was very hesitant and skeptical because my educational background was in electrical engineering and I was a devout Southern Baptist.

I took the MCKS Pranic Healing class and proceeded to practice Pranic Healing on my wife 3 times per day. In 3 weeks, she was walking and in 5 weeks, she was running. This was accomplished without my hands "feeling anything", without being able to feel any energy at all.

The doctor was extremely surprised at my wife's progress, and her family was amazed at how she could be running around with ease and comfort - in light of how severe the injury had been. For this, I am eternally grateful for the Teachings and Blessings of the Teacher.

As a young student, I had an analytical and extremely skeptical mind. My preconceived ideas and deep seated religious beliefs hindered my physical ability to feel energy for four years. Surprisingly, in spite of being physically unable to feel the energies, by simply following the step by step instructions of MCKS, I was able to achieve numerous positive results through applying the principles of Pranic Healing. Despite not feeling energy, I realized the result is not dependent on my sensitivity. All that I had to do is to strictly follow the tried and tested protocols given by MCKS. To my surprise, when I gave up trying to feel the energies, suddenly, my hands began to experience warmth and tingling sensations. Under the guidance of MCKS, I was able to quickly learn how to scan accurately and was able to assist other people who also had difficulty in scanning or feeling energy.

In one Pranic Healing gathering, MCKS introduced Arhatic Yoga. Having read some books on Kundalini, I was very skeptical and decided not to learn this technique due to the possible problems described in those books. However, when MCKS requested another student to invite me to go the Arhatic workshop, I felt internally compelled to attend. In retrospect, it is clear that my soul recognized the magnitude and importance of this opportunity to learn from MCKS - who is a great and revered Teacher in my life.

On one occasion, during an Arhatic retreat after MCKS gave a blessing during the Meditation, I experienced turning into brilliant light and exploding into millions of spiritual light particles. The Teacher transformed into a blinding ball of white light. I felt and saw all the light particles get sucked in and melted into a brilliant ball of light. It was a truly priceless experience.

One time, there was an opportunity for us to learn from another recognized spiritual teacher from India. Many students were flocking to take his darshan, however, within my heart and soul, I knew with great certainty and conviction that MCKS is my primary spiritual teacher (Sat Guru), and he has been for many incarnations.

Both Arhatic Yoga and Pranic Healing have molded my life in every area. I never anticipated these teachings would have had such a profound effect - materially, emotionally, mentally, and spiritually.

MCKS and his teachings have given me inner peace, emotional stability and most importantly, a spiritual purpose. Serving the work of spreading Pranic Healing and other MCKS teachings has given me profound joy, inner satisfaction and the knowledge that I can be an instrument in raising the consciousness of mankind through sharing the brilliance of these Teachings with people throughout the United States.

*A disciple from the Philippines*

## Higher Clairvoyancy

My friend was trying to help my body recover from multiple sclerosis. She heard about Pranic Healing and she took me to a hotel in Santa Monica, C.A. to hear and meet Master Stephen Co who was giving an introduction to Pranic Healing that evening.

At that time, I was a professional psychic who read from tarot cards at an aromatherapy store in West Los Angeles. I was unable to see auras at that time.

After his lecture, I approached Master Co and requested him to give me a healing. When he checked my energy body, by scanning my energy, he said this will take longer than 10 minutes and he recommended that we schedule an appointment.

I went for my first healing treatment in Pasadena one week later. I had been on Ditrapan medication for five years. This was to enhance the ability to control my bladder. After this first healing, it was no longer necessary to take this medication, and I was able to walk more easily, with less shaking.

Amazingly, on the day following the healing, I had green pus oozing out of my navel. Several years previously, I had had a laparoscopy that had never properly healed. This was the beginning of my physical body feeling very much better. After this, other amazing changes began to transpire in my life.

After several healing sessions, I asked Master Co what are all of the little flames I see on top of people's heads. He was really surprised at my question and he asked me to repeat it. He asked me how I had obtained this information and recommended I take Arhatic Yoga. This was the first indication that my higher clairvoyance was being activated.

Additionally, I left a toxic relationship. Then, I flew to Palm Beach, Florida to heal a long time estrangement with my parents.

Because of my newly enhanced intuitive ability, I was able to detect that someone was observing me during a layover between my flights. I called my sister and told her that something wonderful was going to happen.

Once onboard the plane, I received another impression that there was a mechanical problem with the plane. I approached the stewardess and told her to tell the pilot that there was something wrong with the plane. I told her that it could not be fixed and that the pilot should just change the plane.

The pilot came to the passenger cabin and rudely told me that nothing was wrong with the plane. At that moment, a mechanic came onto the plane and informed the pilot that there was something wrong with the plane and that everyone had to deplane and change to another aircraft.

Later, the man who had been observing me in the airport, said he was very attracted to my energy. After our four hour conversation during the plane ride, he decided he wanted to do a documentary regarding healing and alternative realities. He gave me a bank check in order to create a production company for this purpose.

A year and a half later, I saw a young boy working clairvoyantly and assisting a medical doctor at a hospital. I knew if this kid could see auras and help people in this way, I could also see auras. I strongly felt that I would become a professional higher clairvoyant.

In 1998, I took Arhatic Yoga. This changed my perception of everything. I struggled with my personality and my subtle bodies, of which I was previously unaware. A short time after attending a class with MCKS, I felt the presence of a divine Being. I had a profound spiritual awakening. After that, I stopped eating meat completely and immediately. My inner perception shifted to a more universal awareness of the suffering of mankind. I realized the necessity of maintaining a close connection to my Spiritual Teacher, MCKS, and his disciple Stephen Co.

The first time I took the Higher Clairvoyance course with MCKS, I kept looking and looking but did not see anything.

Then, all of a sudden, the light became so intense that it hurt my eyes. Surprisingly, my physical eyes were even bloodshot.

I gave MCKS a reading. When I brought out the tarot cards, he told me I did not need the cards. He reminded me of my lineage. My great, great grandfather was a Kabbalist, and was the chief rabbi of Transylvania. MCKS suggested that I tune into a higher frequency. This was the beginning of my being able to "move out" of my solar plexus center and to read from my higher energy centers.

Two months later, I took a workshop with Master Co who had just returned from a retreat with MCKS. We were sleeping at the house of some friends, who were also taking the workshop. One of them did an invocation to MCKS and the Higher Beings. I saw an angel on fire. I heard the name, Michael. Then, I was lead to open the door to the closet where the furnace was located. I told my friends to open all of the windows and requested them to call the gas company. Because it was very late, they were reluctant to do so, but my husband convinced them to listen. When the gas man entered the house, he immediately turned the unit off, shutting it down. He stated that we would have either died from carbon monoxide poisoning, or would have been blown up by the furnace, which was ready to ignite. He said it was a textbook example of a disaster waiting to happen.

If I had not been involved in Pranic Healing, I would never have known how to look. I felt my purpose in this life had been aligned, because I know why I am here, what my purpose is and that to be healed, I must serve other people. The best way to do this is through practicing the Teachings of MCKS.

Another time, after being with MCKS, I was doing a reading for an actress, a cancer survivor. She had just returned from a full body scan and had been given an all clear signal. But her father, who had died 10 years previously, "spoke" to me and stated that the cancer was still in her uterus. I gave her the father's message. She went back to her medical doctor, and the condition was confirmed. Later, she was completely healed, and had a baby after one and one half years.

After practicing clairvoyance for several years, I was shown a vision of being in an airplane flying between two buildings. People were hysterical. These two buildings were located in New York City. I went to two disciples of MCKS for several months begging them to warn him. They dismissed my visions. Reoccurring dreams continued for nearly a year prior to the actual date. The night of 10 September 2001, I e-mailed another friend a part of this troubling dream.

At 5 a.m. on the morning of September 11th, I awakened my husband and told him "the wolf had been unleashed" and the airplanes hit the twin towers - we were in the west coast, in California and the time corresponded to the time of the disaster on the east coast. When we found out, I called the disciples and screamed at them and told them, if they had told MCKS, we believed the disaster could have been prevented. I was very angry no one believed me. I decided to quit Pranic Healing and no longer wanted to be a clairvoyant. The world was in shock from the event. I had no one with whom I could discuss the extreme trauma of having carried the burden of these visions and dreams.

After that "people" would come to me at night to look for their babies. "Firemen" would come to me in dreams and want me to take them to their children. This was an incredibly painful and difficult time.

Once I recovered from my naive anger, I realized that there was nothing I could have done that could have prevented this terrible event. Nothing anyone could have done could have prevented this from occurring.

I experimented with other forms of spiritual practice and did self study. My life was filled with challenges mentally, emotionally, financially, and spiritually.

I fractured my tail bone in a freak fall and needed healing. Master Co and MCKS both healed me. I gradually became strongly reconnected to Pranic Healing. MCKS also helped me and my husband in our relationship. I felt less judgmental toward other disciples, and realized that Teachers are not perfect, but that they are more evolved than I am. I realized that it is best to decide to forego unnecessary mental criticisms toward other beings. I returned to my work with deeper understanding.

After a healing with MCKS, I had a dream that I was an Egyptian, in an Egyptian temple with other Egyptian priests. Everything in the temple, including all of those present was very light blue in color. Only the outline of hieroglyphics along the wall were gold, but everything else was light, light blue. MCKS explained to me, that this was a vision from the inner world.

Recently, MCKS worked with me, in order to improve my clairvoyancy for more refined energies. During the class,

MCKS had the students take partners. I was standing without a partner and he said, "I will be your partner; you will get an education from me". He asked me to look at his chakras. There was so much to see, that I didn't know where to begin.

I drew a picture of my impressions - flames, lines, and swirly geometric shapes.

So then he took me before the class and asked me to see the 12th chakra which looks like flames on top of the students' heads.

Then, he brought me back and I then practiced zooming in and out, and he taught me how to look at higher and lower frequencies at will.

Then, I observed that MCKS was sitting in his 12th chakra. Everyone else had point of light or a small flame on top of their head, but *MCKS was sitting on top of and within his 12th chakra and was encased in a huge egg-like flame with energy radiating outward from it in all directions and there was spiritual lightning shooting out of his crown chakra.* There were also green and gold bands and rings encircling his body and it was strongly radiating outward - everywhere.

Previously, I had seen disciples touching the guru's feet during a movie of the Kumbamela. Now I understood that this radiatory energy allowed the disciples to safely access these higher energies of the Teacher.

I requested to be allowed to touch the Teacher's feet. This was permitted. I could not believe the feeling, because the Teacher's feet felt like baby skin I was a little bit afraid of the energy, but thought everything was ok, *until one of the lightning bolts hit me. It affected my eyes. I literally staggered out of the area intoxicated with bliss.*

I thought my body was okay, *but then suddenly, the lights became too bright for my eyes. The energy became so intense, that it felt like my eyes had been sunburned.* I was even unable to open my eyes and had to wear dark glasses. Later, my husband reported that my eyes changed color from their normal light brown color to having a purple ring around the iris.

This sensitive condition of the eyes continued until MCKS healed my eyes, enabling me to open them again. Even now, my eyes remain sensitive, when I am in the Teacher's physical presence.

I'm very happy and grateful that my clairvoyancy has improved tremendously due to the personalized training from MCKS.

*A disciple from the U.S.A.*

## Financial and Spiritual Blessings

When I started spending time with MCKS, it was April 2002. I was a senior executive for a company that was really going down hill. This company had been formed with venture capitalists and was losing 7 figures per month and had accumulative losses of over US $ 100 million.

My wife and I were living in a modest, one-bedroom apartment. My personal life also seemed to be going down with the company. I was in a state of depression.

I met Master Choa in Mumbai on a Tuesday, and he asked if I could be in the United States of America on the following Friday. He thought I might be able to do some business there, to turn things around. I was rather skeptical and thought about going to the U.S. for one day only, as per Master's request.

My personal intuition said, "go, go" and so I followed my intuition and flew to Los Angeles.

Over the next few months, I became more interested in Master's meditations and teachings. This led to my first Prosperity course, on 1 August 2002.

One of the most dramatic, life changing teachings I received, was the complete application of the Concept of Tithing as taught by MCKS. My first success was when I followed Master's instructions and properly decreed after donating $5,000 from my company for charitable purposes. The result was, the following week, our company received $50,000 in outstanding client payments which had been previously stuck for 60 to 90 days. This is 10 times the amount tithed.

Being very analytical, I conducted several experiments on giving to various organizations - including those founded by Master. This was very interesting.

*I found that the return on the spiritual investment created by tithing, was much higher when giving to the charitable organizations founded by Master.*

The second amazing change was that over the next week, month and year - the first three Kriyashakti wishes in that class came true.

These wishes ranged from getting a new client for my company within one week, *to selling my company for the price specified (100 million US dollars), within the time specified, on 8 August 2003.*

Apart from the material and financial blessings, my life began to change as I became happier and more balanced, more focused and effective through using the teachings of MCKS.

As I spent more time meditating and following the teachings, amazingly my circle of influence also increased. For example, everyday, small positive things would happen. I experienced new found peace in myself and in my marriage.

With Master's guidance and blessings, I started working 4 ranks below the level of the CEO of a multi billion dollar company. *Within 24 months, I was promoted to become the youngest senior vice president, ahead of others who had been working in the company for more than 20 years.*

With regular meditation, I was able to achieve greater mental clarity and to make better decisions. Increased intuition developed into greater insights, so that I am now able to see from the personal perspective, from the business perspective and from the world perspective.

My spiritual experiences have been so intense and constant. *During meditation, it is now possible to experience seeing and getting closer to the blue pearl on a regular basis.*

One such miraculous event was for my wife and I to simultaneously see the pillar of light and the blue pearl during the birth of our first daughter.

Recently, I was with 3 other disciples and Master gave a shaktipat or spiritual empowerment. *We heard the inner sound and our consciousness was literally pulled out of our bodies. We experienced oneness with the divine light, expansion of consciousness and intense bliss.*

MCKS' Notes: Financial and Spiritual Blessings come from God, passing through Mahaguruji Mei Ling and the Higher Beings. MCKS is just a humble instrument.

*A disciple from India and the U.S.A.*

## Meeting MCKS in the Inner World

In early November 2005, after traveling for several days with MCKS, we rested at a quiet hotel. The following day, MCKS was scheduled to teach at a local center.

That night, after doing some distant Pranic Healing sessions, at approximately 2 a.m., I began to sense MCKS was meditating in his room which was about 15 feet away from me.

I began to sit in meditation and as I experienced intense bliss and oneness, I felt myself being rapidly transported to many different places in the inner world - one after the other.

I felt I was moving very fast, through several distant worlds, each very unique and far apart.

About an hour later, I physically laid down to rest with the intention of remaining receptive and one with MCKS' consciousness.

A few minutes later my consciousness was pulled out of my body. All perception of my physical body disappeared and there was only divine oneness.

I experienced myself as a being of divine light, and experienced divine oneness.

After being in this state for sometime, which is a state that is difficult to describe, I felt as though I was looking down, seeing myself as a small point of light. There was no physical body. I was simply that point of light.

Although I was physically in the next room, I saw MCKS meditating. He appeared as a very large golden sun.

I experienced that MCKS was inviting his senior disciples and loved ones to come to him.

I observed myself - as the point of light - moving towards MCKS and I felt as though he was inviting and drawing me gently and slowly, closer and closer towards him.

As I approached and entered into the huge Golden Sun, there was a merging and I experienced my consciousness expanding in all directions, experiencing divine oneness and experiencing God saturating every part of me. It felt as if I, the soul, was everywhere simultaneously.

This experience continued for sometime and then later, I slowly returned to my body.

After about 4 a.m., I felt as though he was finished meditating and that he had turned his attention to working on other matters. The divine energy and presence of great

Beings in the room with him was extremely intense. This continued until about 6:45 a.m. It was only then that my body could fall asleep.

Then, at 7:30 a.m. I received a phone call saying that MCKS was inviting me for breakfast. I went downstairs and asked, "Master, were you awake all night? Were you meditating between 2 and 4 a.m.?" He said yes to both questions. He confirmed he had meditated about between 2 and 4 a.m. and that he was working between 4 and about 6:45 a.m.

Then, I described my experiences in the night and he smiled, nodded as he listened and said, "Very good, very good".

There have been countless spiritual experiences during the years I have been with MCKS. The teachings and the blessings which gradually bring one to experience our beloved God are beyond all measure and truly priceless.

The constant acts of kindness I have witnessed MCKS do for strangers who are in need and for his students are a living example of the virtue of loving kindness. They have been a constant inspiration to me. Years of traveling with him around the world and receiving his teachings and blessings fill me with joy, gratitude and reverence. Thank you, Master Choa, thank you Lord Mahaguruji Mei Ling and thank you God.

*A disciple from the U.S.A.*

## Gratitude

After a decade of being a science educator in a Catholic university, I recognize that education is not just an information but formation. The student becomes the center of the teaching process and the subject matter is the vehicle to attain such a goal. The power of the teachings depends on the quality of the teacher and his effectivity in influencing positive changes in the lives of the students and collectively brings forth societal transformation.

I felt this essence of education when I attended the basic Pranic Healing seminar conducted in our school in November 1990, attended by the whole faculty and school administration. The seminar opened my heart, inspired my inquisitive mind and provided a comprehensive explanation to my inner experiences with invisible beings which I have had as early as a young child. The inner teachings shed light to my innate clairvoyant faculties which had previously disturbed me and caused me to sometimes feel unstable. My own misinterpretations of my experiences were completely healed and transformed into precious gifts of inner healing, inner peace, inner joy, freedom and gratitude.

Pranic Healing gives emphasis and clarity to my soul mission and life's direction. I realized that its teachings and application are an actual expression of the bible message, "Be the light of the world and the salt of the Earth". (Matthew 5:13-14)

The principles and procedures were so simple yet very powerful, grounded, very practical and self-empowering that I strongly affirm the common expression among Pranic Healers, "Pranic Healing is love and compassion in action."

Pranic Healing was adopted by our school clinic, by our medical doctors, nurses and dentists. It is part of our school outreach program that tremendously reduced our school's medical expenses and minimized absenteeism. The lessons on character building and Meditation on Twin Hearts were integrated in our classes. This positively influenced our students' discipline.

The Pranic Healing guidelines and practices were used to illustrate abstract scientific laws in my chemistry and physics classes, facilitating a clearer understanding of the interconnectedness of all creation and the perfect combination of science and spirituality. This balanced our students' development.

In July 1991, a killer earthquake struck the Philippines. It strongly shook our three storey school building. Amazingly, the school community remained calm. The school directress played the Meditation on Twin Hearts and requested the school community to focus on their crown chakra while the students went out of the building in perfect order. No stampede, no panic - everybody was safe and the school building remained in perfect shape. That was a miracle!

As I carried out my Pranic Healing mission which I integrated in my teaching career, I recognized the significance of these teachings. As part of the school curriculum, the teachings serves as a great vehicle for educators' formation, for dynamic, creative and spiritual leadership. Healthy teachers build healthy students.

I was so inspired, so in love with Pranic Healing, that I decided to work full time as a Pranic Healing instructor with the World Pranic Healing Foundation (WPHF) in April 1992.

The WPHF was founded and is guided by our strong-willed teacher and founder GMCKS. He has great insights and a clear vision. WPHF's mandate is to spread MCKS Pranic Healing and Arhatic Yoga to developing countries. It began in a very small office at Cubao, Quezon City. There was only a table and chair and no telephone. Piles of books served as the trainers' seat and table during meetings. Pranic Healing gained momentum as it continued to carry out its noble mission to help alleviate the suffering of people in the Philippines and in the developing countries.

As WPHF's coverage widened, a new office was opened then in 1991 the office transferred to a building in Makati. It was so magnetic that larger numbers of students came in and in 1992, it was necessary to be moved to another larger office in Makati City, where we remained until 1998. Progress continued and we transferred to a larger office in 1999 to Ortigas, Pasig City. Finally, we moved to our present beautiful office in the Medical Plaza Ortigas, San Miguel Ave., Pasig City.

In my opinion, it's not just the message but the messenger, not just the teachings but the teacher and not just the subject matter that matters most but the energy that goes with the subject matter.

*A disciple from the Philippines*

## The Mission

In 1991, I had a deep desire to commit myself to a life in the missions and so I entered a convent to become a nun. There was such a deep longing to do greater service.

I was already a postulant nun when a nun invited me to join an introductory class on Pranic Healing. It was very enlightening, but I was suffering from a very bad long-standing migraine. Amazingly, I was healed instantaneously. This made me very interested in learning Pranic Healing. I joined the MCKS Pranic Healing workshop immediately.

I was able to receive answers to my questions and felt empowered to take care of my health needs for myself and my loved ones. I had an intense desire to meet MCKS and to learn more from him directly.

I first met MCKS in January 1991, and was fortunate to learn Advanced Pranic Healing directly from him. Upon meeting him, I felt as though I had known him for a long, long time. What struck me was the practicality of the teachings that can be easily applied to my everyday life. This was the beginning of my inner transformation. I began to realize that I would be able to help other people by being able to heal them. I thought that becoming involved with Pranic Healing would give me a positive way to express my mission. I was very attracted to the work and was inspired to organize Pranic Healing workshops regularly. What inspired me to move forward was my wonderful experiences and also being able to help others miraculously transform their lives.

By August of 1991, I was invited to become a full-time Pranic Healing instructor. This was the beginning of an interesting period. From being a postulant nun I went into spreading Pranic Healing and was assigned to teach in provincial areas of the Philippines.

What touched me about doing this work was being able to "multiply" myself, to teach people in remote areas how to take care of their own health needs, and to watch them evolve. I love "living" in the community of strangers whom I had never met - experiencing different expressions of life in all of their color and flavor. We went into new areas where Pranic Healing was yet unrecognized. It was always amazing to see the magical effect of Pranic Healing, changing and uplifting so many lives - including my own.

The effect of Pranic Healing in my family was wonderful. Our family relationships - parents, brother and sisters - were strengthened and sustained. Healing old wounds, healing my father from his long term smoking habit (he began at age 13 and smoked for more than 50 years!), the healing of our family finances (now money flows easily into our family) and the realization that life is much easier now. Another wonderful thing is that there have been no major sicknesses in our family - and I feel that divine protection is embracing our entire family regularly.

I recognize this to be a strong motivation for me to do this work. Because we help other people, and spread the work of Pranic Healing, I believe that Divine Grace protects and sustains me and my family.

*A disciple from the Philippines*

Chapter 18

# The Existence Of God Is Self-Evident



## Path of Knowledge and Understanding

Yoga means spiritual oneness. What is spiritual oneness? Spiritual oneness means the incarnated soul is achieving a higher degree of oneness with the higher soul, and a certain degree of oneness with God and oneness with All.

There are many paths to achieving illumination and spiritual oneness. One of the paths is the Yoga of Knowledge and Understanding. This is called Jnana Yoga. This path is the easiest path for those who are mentally developed. By reading this book just once, the spiritual cord will become much bigger. There will be a greater downpour of spiritual energy. The crown chakra and all of the other chakras will become bigger. These effects are temporary. It is necessary to repeatedly read this book over and over again; a person can rapidly achieve illumination and divine oneness within a short period of time. The time factor may vary from several years to a lifetime. One lifetime is still considered short because other yogis take many incarnations just to achieve this state.

The Yoga of Knowledge and Understanding also requires physical purification and inner purification - character building. Without physical purification the body may become sick. Without inner purification, the meditator may become psychologically imbalanced. It is also important to generate good karma by doing service and tithing, in order to offset one's ancient negative karma.

The original title was called Spiritual Findings. Through many years of Arhatic Yoga experiments, inner experiences, the use of mental, intuitive and higher intelligence and inner transmission; many important "spiritual findings" can be concluded. Arhatic Yoga is a system of advanced spiritual practices.

The title was changed to "The Existence of God is Self-Evident" since this is one of the most important Spiritual Findings.

God's Blessing be with you in your search for Spiritual Truth.

# I AM THAT I AM

I AM not the body.
The body is the vehicle
of the Soul.

I AM not the emotion.
I AM not the thought.
The carpenter is not the furniture.
The emotions and the thoughts
are products of the Soul.

I AM not the mind.
The computer user is not the computer.
The mind is only a subtle
instrument of the Soul.
I AM the Soul.

I AM a spiritual being of
Divine Intelligence,
Divine Love, Divine Power.
I AM one with my Higher Soul;
I AM THAT I AM.

I AM one with my Divine Spark.
I AM a Child of God.
I AM connected with God.
I AM one with God.
I AM one with All.

Spiritual Findings

1. Spiritual energy is needed for expansion of consciousness and traveling in the inner worlds. Stillness and awareness are not enough. No spiritual energy, no expansion of consciousness. Spiritual empowerment or Shaktipat is the transference of tremendous spiritual energy to enable the consciousness of the disciple to be able to travel to the different levels of the inner world. This transference of tremendous spiritual energy is called initiation in modern esoteric books.

2. Principle of Omnipresence. Based on inner experiences and experiments, consciousness travels infinitely faster than the speed of light and in all directions. One experiences a certain degree of Omnipresence. Different levels of consciousness travel at different speeds.

   Although the broadcasting tower is in one place, the signal is Omnipresent within certain radius. The radius of the Omnipresence depends on the power of the broadcasting tower. God is Omnipresent. The soul is Omnipresent up to a certain radius depending on how much spiritual power it has.

3. Inner stillness is not the ultimate objective. It is just a stepping stone to greater inner activities which manifest as partial functioning of intuitive and higher intelligence, illumination and/or expansion of consciousness.

4. A disciple may experience *oneness* with the "light" and expansion of consciousness. In many instances a disciple may not even reach the outer edge of the "light" within one incarnation.

5. Before the "light", there is the dark void. The inner world consists of a series of greater "light" and dark void. This dark void seems to be transition realm between two worlds or realms of "light".

6. Within the "brilliant light" is the "form": the planets and the moons, the sun, the galaxies, the universe and the universes. Please note that the word *universes* is in plural form. God being God cannot just create one universe. God being God continuously creates countless universes.

7. Within the "light" are Great, Great Beings whose existence and functions are incomprehensible to common people and even to most disciples.

8. Principle of Now. During deep meditation, sometimes the meditator may experience a state of consciousness that is called Now, where the past, present and future are experienced as One or Now.

   To understand this concept, it must be specified that the experience of Now is not static but dynamic. The present is constantly becoming the past and the immediate future is constantly becoming the present. And the distant future is dynamic.

The future that is being experienced at that moment is not static. It is dynamic. To comprehend this concept of Now, imagine that there are one million super computers connected and gridded together. The super computers have built-in programs. All data have already been inputted and the moment the new data are encoded, the gridded super computers* would almost instantaneously come out with the projected future outcome or events.

The past, the present and the future are experienced simultaneously.

9. Creation is not a one time process. The process of creation is continuous, directed and evolutionary. Creation and evolution are two sides of the same coin. The proper term that should be used is "Evolutionary Creation".

10. The *inner sound* is continuously used in the process of creation. Therefore, creation is a continuous process. In some religious texts this sound is called the *Word*.

11. Great spiritual Beings, great spiritual Teachers and their disciples are *spiritual energy transformers.*

* A grid computer is a **large number** of same class, self-contained computers which are clustered together through a super fast network. As a grid computer, it can calculate faster than the same number of computers calculating individually. A sophisticated operating system takes care of the (load) sharing in computing and processing.

Reference: "Grid Computer", The History of Computing Foundation, 2000. http://www.thop.net, http://www-1.ibm.net.

In the beginning was the Word,
and the Word was with God,
and the Word was God.

John 1:1

In the beginning was Brahman,
with whom was the Word;
and the Word
was truly
the Supreme Brahman.

Rig Veda

12. The world consists of a *series of spiritual energy transformers*. The planet Earth is an energy transformer, the sun is an energy transformer, the constellation and galaxy are energy transformers. Our universe is a spiritual energy transformer, and a megauniverse is an energy transformer. A megauniverse consists probably of billions of universes.

13. Spiritual energy transformers are capable of stepping down or stepping up the energy. Spiritual energy transformers also qualify, modify or transform the energy passing through them.

14. Coexisting and interpenetrating physical objects and non-physical objects, is *pure energy with consciousness*. This pure energy with consciousness is called *Nothingness*, *Ain*, *Sunya* or *Kung* in different religions.

15. From the Absolute Supreme God comes Pure Energy with Consciousness and Pure Matter. Pure Energy with Consciousness is called "light" in Genesis. Pure matter is called "darkness" in Genesis. The combination of these two results in creation. In India, the word purusha means consciousness. It actually means pure energy with consciousness. Mulaprakriti literally means root matter. Root matter means pure matter. What we call energy is not pure energy. What we call matter is not pure matter. What we call "energy" and "matter", is actually composed of Pure Energy with Consciousness and Pure Matter.

16. Through intuitive and higher intelligence, it can be sensed that the universe is undergoing a series of expansion and contraction, a series of creation and destruction.

17. The Supreme God is the All Pervasive Energy with Consciousness. This All Pervasive Energy is very subtle and almost imperceptible. It is super stable at the same time all powerful. It does not have form. This Supreme Being or Universal Pervasive Intelligent Energy is what we call the Supreme God who is formless. This is how MCKS experiences the Supreme God.

18. In Judaism, there is no image of the Supreme God. In the Christian religion, there is also no image of the Supreme God. In Islam, the Supreme God has no image. In the Hindu tradition, the Parabrahman does not have any form. In Taoism, Tao is formless.

19. Since most people cannot comprehend God in this manner, it was necessary for the great spiritual teachers to create images for the different aspects of God.

20. Principle of Individuality and the Principle of Oneness. Individuality and Spiritual Oneness coexist simultaneously. Within spiritual oneness exists individuality. Within individuality exists spiritual oneness. These paradoxical truths coexist simultaneously.

Imagine there are one million computers. Each computer is an individual computer but when connected and gridded together, they function as One Mega Computer.

The energy body of the planet Earth has a consciousness of its own. The Earth's energy body is actually a Great Living Planetary Computer. Your energy body and its chakras has a consciousness of its own and is a living mini biocomputer. It is connected with the Great Planetary Biocomputer. The task is to access the Great Planetary Biocomputer. The whole universe or universes has consciousness and is a Great Living Cosmic Computer. This is just one level of truth. The Principle of Interconnectedness and Principle of Oneness have different levels of Truth.

The reason why these Spiritual Teachings are correlated with modern science is to make them more comprehensible.

21. Based on the Principle of Spiritual Oneness, whatever a person does to others he does to himself. Spiritually, the causes set within the inner world will inevitably materialize physically unless a neutralizing factor is set in motion. The fruits may be pleasant or unpleasant depending on the nature of the seed that was planted. This is called the Law of Karma.

22. There is only one Supreme God who is Omnipresent. The presence of God in the planet

Earth is called the Planetary God or the Planetary Parabrahman. The Planetary God is also called Planetary Logos since life on the Planet Earth, physical and non-physical, is sustained through the constant use of the *Sound* or the *Word*.

23. The Planetary Logos is a part of the Supreme God and is spiritually one with the Supreme God. Therefore, there is only *One God*.

24. The Presence of the Supreme God, in the sun and in the solar system is called the Solar God. In the Indian tradition, the Solar Parabrahman is called Lord Surya or Lord Savitur. In the Egyptian tradition, Amen Ra. Ra means Sun. Amen Ra means the Solar God.

25. The Solar God is also called the Solar Logos. Since the existence of the sun, the planets and their moons are sustained through the constant use of the Sound or the Word.

26. The Solar Logos was referred to by St. Paul when he said, "He is not far from us; for in Him, we live, and move, and have our being". (Acts 17:27-28)

27. The presence of the Supreme God in our galaxy is called the Galactic Logos or the Galactic Parabrahman.

    The Golden Age occurs when our solar system is nearest to the center of the galaxy, nearest to the Galactic Logos. The Dark Age occurs when it is farthest away.* This truth have been taught by the Great Spiritual Teachers.

Spiritual Evolution is governed by the Law of Cycles.

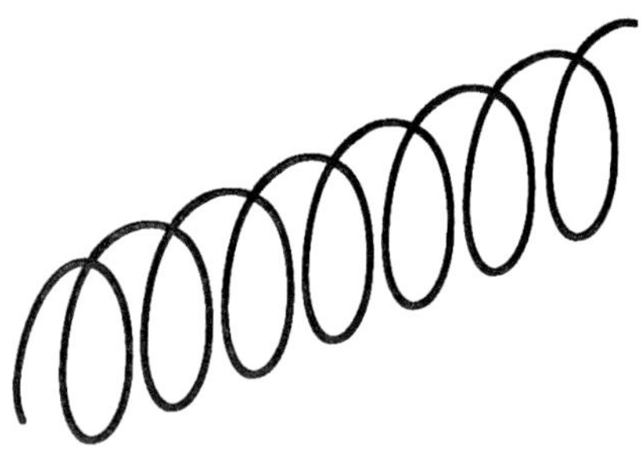

It is cyclical but on an upward trend.

28. The Universal Logos or Universal Parabrahman for our universe.

29. The Cosmic Logos or the Cosmic Parabrahman for the universes.

30. Finally, the Absolute Supreme God, the Causeless Cause, the Source from which all comes from.

31. Spiritually, all of the different Logos are parts and one with the Absolute Supreme God. Therefore, there is only One God - the Absolute Supreme God.

32. A country has a national government, state government, and city government. There is a

* This great truth has been recently clarified by Sri Yukteswar Giri, in his book, The Holy Science, 1894.

hierarchy of governments. Likewise, there are different levels of manifestation of the Supreme God.

33. The Avatars, the Buddhas, Boddhisattvas, Messiahs, Prophets or the Messengers of God come from the Planetary Logos or the Planetary Parabrahman.

34. The Absolute Supreme God is Omnipotent which manifests as God the Will. Will is divided into purpose and power. Purpose without power is impotence. Power without a purpose is not power since it will be diffused and scattered.

35. The Absolute Supreme God is Omniprovident. To love is to provide. To provide is to preserve.

36. The Absolute Supreme God is Omniscient. This manifests as God the Creator.

37. God and the Holy Trinity can be understood as the invisible "light" passing through a prism producing seven colors. Of the seven colors, three are primary colors which, when combined, produce the invisible "light".

38. These three aspects of the Supreme God manifest down to the Planetary Logos.

39. In Christian religion, these three aspects of the Planetary Logos are known as:

    God the Father - God the Will
    God the Son - God the Love
    God the Holy Spirit - God the Creator

40. Which is different from:

The Father - The Divine Spark
The Son - The I AM, The Higher Soul
The Holy Spirit - The Incarnated Soul

This is why St. Paul said, "...your body is a temple of the Holy Spirit". (1 Corinthians 6:19) What He meant is that the body is the temple or the vehicle of the incarnated soul.

41. In the Indian tradition, the Holy Trinity is composed of:

God Shiva: The Destroyer and Restorer
God Vishnu: The Provider
God Brahma: The Creator

42. God the Omnipotent is called God Shiva, who is the Destroyer and Restorer. To destroy and to restore is equal to regeneration. The word regeneration has many meanings including spiritual evolution.

When the body is destroyed or dies, the soul is liberated. It reincarnates in another body. This is the meaning of Restoration or Resurrection. Through this process the soul gradually evolves.

Regeneration or creative destruction can be applied to a house which is called remodeling. Creative destruction when applied to the human body is called regeneration. In a company, this is called reformulating the strategy and policies, and restructuring the organization. In a country, this is called progressive policies and progressive laws. In relation to the human race, it is called planetary spiritual evolution.

43. God the Omniprovident is called God Vishnu, who is the Preserver. As stated earlier, to love is to provide, and to provide is to preserve. In relation to parents, it means earning a living; providing shelter, food for the family, and education for the children. In relation to the government, the act of providing and preserving is called the "social security system".

In relation to the Spiritual Teacher, it is providing spiritual teaching, moral values, and spiritual practices to preserve the students from morally degenerating and improving their life in general.

44. God the Omniscient is called God Brahma, who is the Creator. God is all-knowing. God being God cannot manifest as sterile intelligence. God manifests as active intelligence, as creative intelligence; therefore, God is not only Omniscient, God is the creator.

45. God the Creator is called God the Holy Spirit in the Christian tradition and God Brahma, in the Hindu tradition. God the Holy Spirit or God Brahma is the Divine Mother.

You cannot ask the husband to produce a baby. It has to be the wife who produces the baby. It has to be the mother.

46. In the Islam tradition, some of the different aspects of God are known as the 99 names of Allah.

47. Human beings made in the image of God, also have the three qualities:

    - Will
    - Love
    - Intelligence

    These three qualities exist in every person in varying degrees of development.

48. There are saints, yogis, and lay people who have experienced oneness with God. Qualitatively this is true. Quantitatively this is true to a very minute degree. Truth must be understood qualitatively and quantitatively.

    These saints, yogis, and lay people, if they were to achieve a high degree of oneness with the Planetary Logos, their bodies would die instantly. How much more for the Solar Logos? How much more for the Absolute Supreme God?

    The Planetary Logos told Moses, "You cannot see my face, for no one may see me and live". (Exodus 33:20)

    There are very few exceptions to this rule and MCKS is not one of the few exceptions.

49. The soul, its subtle vehicles and its physical body, must be given very minute dosage of intense

spiritual energy, of very minute dosage of oneness with God. The capacity of the soul and its vehicles, and its physical body must be gradually developed. Too much intense divine energy, too much divine oneness may cause the body to become sick, to become permanently damaged or to die.

50. Based on the Principle of Interconnectedness and Principle of Oneness, one can have access to Power, Love and Intelligence. Quantitatively, this is true to a minute degree. Even this minute access and minute dosages of Divine Power, Divine Love and Divine Intelligence manifest as incredible phenomena called miracles by the masses.

St. Augustine said, "Miracles do not happen in contradiction to nature, but to that which is known to us about nature."*

51. The existence of God is self-evident. It is amazing that those who have eyes do not see. The existence of a camera factory is self-evident by the existence of the camera. The existence of God is self-evident, by the existence of the eye, which is infinitely more complicated than a camera.

The existence of a computer factory is self-evident by the existence of the computer. The existence of God is self-evident by the existence of the brain, which is infinitely more complex than the most advanced computer.

* Master Choa Kok Sui, Miracles Through Pranic Healing, 3rd ed. (Philippines, Institute for Inner Studies, Inc., 1997).

A machine is produced based on the design and mathematical computations made by engineers. These mathematical computations are based on mathematical formulas. The universe is designed and governed by certain Laws of Nature, which are expressed in mathematical formulas. Who else but the Supreme God, who is Omniscient, could do this? Just as the existence of mathematical formulas to compute interest payments, amortization, principal repayments, and others, implies the existence of intelligence. The existence of mathematical formulas, which design and govern the universe, implies the existence of God, who is OmniIntelligent. This Truth is obvious, yet many do not see this obvious Truth.

52. A beautiful rose is made of only four physical ingredients:

    a. water
    b. trace minerals
    c. air
    d. sunlight

    Only God can make something so complex, so beautiful, with just these four physical ingredients. Scientists, even if given trillions of U.S. dollars, will not be able to produce a rose just with these four physical ingredients.

53. The flowers, the fruits, the plants, and the trees, are produced with these four physical ingredients. To produce chemicals you need chemical factories, chemists, and chemical engineers. Many of the

biochemicals in the flowers, in the fruits, in the plants and in the trees cannot be reproduced by the biochemists and the chemical engineers. Yet a plant or a tree, which is not managed and controlled by biochemists and chemical engineers and which is much smaller than a chemical factory, produces them. Truly God is OmniIntelligent. Truly God is Omnipotent. Nature is God's factory. To see nature is to see the creation of God. The existence of God is self-evident!

54. MCKS has experienced God's love. We are all children of God. God loves all of us. God loves the good, the not so good, the bad, and the terrible. God loves us no matter what we are. God is all loving. God is all merciful.

55. Divine Justice can be balanced by Divine Mercy. It is in forgiving that one is forgiven. "It is in pardoning that we are pardoned," said St. Francis of Assisi. By showing mercy, one can receive mercy. "Blessed are the merciful for Mercy shall be shown to them". (Matthew 5:7) If a person does not show mercy by forgiving, how can one harvest forgiveness, thereby partially erasing one's negative karma? The Law of Forgiveness and the Law of Mercy supersede the Law of Karma.

It is with great reluctance that this subject matter has been revealed. It is possible that most readers may not be able to comprehend most of the spiritual findings and may consider all of these as pure nonsense.

## MCKS

Some readers or students might create an unrealistic image of what MCKS is, based on their preconceived idea of what a spiritual teacher should be. All of these, MCKS is not. MCKS is just a good person who is trying to be a better person - a better soul. MCKS, just like all of you, is in the process of evolving and has to repeatedly practice patience, understanding and tolerance. MCKS also gets hurt and experiences pain and has to remember to practice forgiveness. MCKS is as human as all of you.

## Discernment

A student must practice discernment. Do not believe a statement to be true just because "someone said so". Do not believe something to be true because "someone" claims information has been received through "inner transmission".

Use discernment. Do not believe something to be true, just because MCKS said so. Practice Arhatic Yoga diligently. Validate the truth for yourself. Use intelligent evaluation. If the student is not in a position to validate the truth as of the moment, then he should check at least the track record of the teacher. Have the previous teachings of the teacher been validated? If yes, then the other teachings may be considered to be tentative truth for the moment, until the student is in a position to validate them for himself.

Lord Buddha and the Great Spiritual Teachers have repeatedly taught their students to practice discernment or intelligent evaluation.

Peace be with you.

God's Blessings be with you
and your family.

Blessings of the
Lord Mahaguruji Mei Ling
and all the Great Ones
be with all of you.

M.C.K.S.

# Appendices

A

## Master Choa Kok Sui Tapes and CDs

Meditation on Twin Hearts for Peace and Illumination

Meditation on Twin Hearts with Self-Healing

Meditation on the Soul

Meditation on Twin Hearts
for Psychological Health and Well-Being

Meditation on Loving Kindness

Planetary Meditation for Peace

Wesak Festival Meditation

Om: The Sound of Stillness

Om Shanti

Om Mani Padme Hum
Mantra of Compassion and Mercy

Meditation on the Lord's Prayer:
Universal and Kabbalistic Versions

Arhatic Yoga Kundalini Meditation:
Meditation on the Inner Breath
(for Arhatic Yogis only)

Arhatic Dhyan
(for Arhatic Yogis only)

**B**

## Master Choa Kok Sui Courses

1. Pranic Healing
2. Advanced Pranic Healing
3. Pranic Psychotherapy
4. Pranic Crystal Healing
5. Pranic Self-Healing
6. Pranic Psychic Self-Defense
7. Kriyashakti for Prosperity and Success
8. Achieving Oneness with the Higher Soul
9. Arhatic Yoga
10. Arhatic Sexual Alchemy
11. Clairvoyance
12. Pranic Feng Shui
13. Meditation on the Lord's Prayer
14. Spiritual Business Management
15. Spiritual Essence of Man
16. Om Mani Padme Hum
17. Christianity Revealed
18. Buddhism Revealed



For more information, contact:
**INSTITUTE FOR INNER STUDIES, INC.**
*Postal Address:* Suite 808 G/F Island Plaza Salcedo Bldg.
105 Leviste St., Salcedo Village
1227 Makati City, Philippines
Tel. Nos. (63-2) 819-18-74; 812-2326; 813-2562
Fax No. (63-2) 731-38-28
E-mail: gmcks_iis@yahoo.com
Website: www.pranichealing.org

*For certificates, licenses, books, tapes, compact discs, and aura spray you can order at:* **iis_order@yahoo.com**

# C

## Pranic Healing Centers and Organizations

**Institute for Inner Studies, Inc.**
*Postal Address:* Suite 808 G/F Island Plaza
Salcedo Bldg., 105 Leviste St., Salcedo Village
1227 Makati City, Philippines
Tel. Nos. (63-2) 819-1874; 812-2326; 813-2562
Fax No. (63-2) 731-3828
E-mail: gmcks_iis@yahoo.com
Website: www.pranichealing.org

**World Pranic Healing Foundation**
Unit 2210 Medical Plaza Ortigas Condominium
San Miguel Avenue, Ortigas Center, Pasig City 1605
Metro Manila Philippines
or
P.O. Box 3521 Makati Central Post Office
Makati City 1275, Philippines
Tel. Nos. (63-2) 635-9732 to 34
Fax No. (63-2) 687-4726
E-mail: wphf@iconn.com.ph
Website:www.worldpranichealing.com

**Planetary Peace Movement (PPM)**
International Headquarters
Suite 117 G/F Island Plaza Salcedo Bldg.
105 Leviste St., Salcedo Village
1227 Makati City, Philippines
Tel. No. +(61-7) 5545-2333/ +(63)916-649-8300
Fax No. +(617) 5545-3337
E-mail: omlove@aol.com
Website: www.meditatepeace.com

## Pranic Healing International Addresses

Pranic Healing services and courses are available in pranic healing centers and organizations of the countries listed below.

For specific addresses, contact numbers, and the complete, updated country list, visit the website:

**www.pranichealing.org**

ARGENTINA
AUSTRALIA
AUSTRIA
BELGIUM
BELIZE
BENIN
BOLIVIA
BOSNIA-HERZEGOVINA
BRAZIL
BULGARIA
CANADA
CARIBBEAN Region
CHILE
COLOMBIA
COSTA RICA
CROATIA
CYPRUS
CZECH REPUBLIC
DOMINICAN REPUBLIC
ECUADOR
EL SALVADOR
FIJI
FINLAND
FRANCE
GERMANY
GHANA
GREECE
GUATEMALA
GUYANA
HONDURAS
HONG KONG
HUNGARY
INDIA
INDONESIA
IRAN
IRELAND
ISRAEL
ITALY
JAPAN
JORDAN
KAZAKHSTAN
KENYA
LEBANON
LITHUANIA
MALAYSIA
MAURITIUS
MEXICO
The NETHERLANDS
NEW ZEALAND
NICARAGUA
NIGERIA
OMAN
PANAMA
PARAGUAY
PERU
PHILIPPINES
POLAND
PORTUGAL
PUERTO RICO
ROMANIA
RUSSIA
SCOTLAND
SINGAPORE
SLOVAKIA
SLOVENIA
SOUTH AFRICA
SPAIN
SRI LANKA
SWEDEN
SWITZERLAND
SYRIA
THAILAND
TOGO
TURKEY
UKRAINE
UNITED ARAB EMIRATES
UNITED KINGDOM
UNITED STATES of AMERICA
URUGUAY
VENEZUELA
WEST AFRICA

# Index

# A

## D

## E

## H



## I

## N



## O

## P

## R

## S